DEAD MEAT

DEAD MEAT

Sue Coe

Introduction by
ALEXANDER COCKBURN

FOUR WALLS EIGHT WINDOWS
New York / London

F O R   T H E   A N I M A L S

Published in the United States by: Four Walls Eight Windows
39 West 14th Street, room 503, New York, N.Y., 10011

U.K. offices:
Four Walls Eight Windows/Turnaround
27 Horsell Road, London, N51 XL, England

First printing January 1996.

Library of Congress Cataloging-in-Publication Data:
    Coe, Sue, 1951-
    Dead meat/by Sue Coe: introduction by Alexander Cockburn
       p.   cm.
    ISBN 1-56858-041-X
    1. Coe, Sue, 1951- Political and social views. 2. Meat industry and trade
in art. I. Title.
    N6797.C55A35   1995
    759.2—dc20 95   35536
                    CIP

10 9 8 7 6 5 4 3 2 1

Book design by Cindy LaBreacht
Original artwork photographed by D. James Dee
Printed in the United States

PAGE II: ILLUSTRATION #6652

ACKNOWLEDGMENTS

The following slaughterhouse journals are the result of six years of work, traveling around the country to various meatpacking plants. In the early 20th century, when Upton Sinclair wrote *The Jungle*, packinghouses were very proud of their slaughtering techniques and would offer guided tours for the public to show off the new technology. By the end of the 20th century, that is no longer the case. The public is not welcome. Slaughterhouses, especially the larger ones, are guarded like military compounds, and it is almost impossible to gain access. I usually got in by knowing someone, who knew someone else, who had a business relationship with the plant or slaughterhouse. There were times when I made an official appointment months in advance, only to arrive and be denied admission. The use of a camera was usually forbidden, and video cameras were out of the question. A sketchbook, however, was usually considered harmless.

I've changed the names of some of the slaughterhouses to protect the workers. In one case, the owner threatened to kill me if I ever published the name of that slaughterhouse. There were a few slaughterhouse bosses and producers of meat who went out of their way to be helpful and paid me every courtesy. They understood the contradictions of what they were doing and were willing to reveal the concealed industry and open up the debate.

I'd like to thank Lorri and Gene Bauston at Farm Sanctuary, Mandy Coe, Steve Murray, John Carlin, JillEllyn Riley, Judy Brody, Gary Francione, Anna Charlton, Hildegard Bachart, Jane Kallir, Carl Johnson, Helene Klodawsky, Art Spiegelman, François Mouly, Rachel Rosenthal, Peter Wolf, Eric Avery, Paul Marcus, John Garfield, Amelita Donald, Steve Heller, Chris Carter, and Jim Ann Howard.

CONTENTS

BROILER HARVESTER

THE BURDEN OF COMPLICITY

Tom Regan

> As often as Herman had witnessed the slaughter of animals and fish, he always had the same thought: in their behavior toward creatures, all men were Nazis. The smugness with which man could do with other species as he pleased exemplified the most extreme racist theories, the principle that might is right.—Isaac Bashevis Singer, *Enemies: A Love Story*

Among the members of the human family we recognize the moral imperative of respect. Every human is a somebody, not a something. Morally disrespectful treatment occurs when those who stand at the power end of a power relationship treat the less powerful as if they were mere objects. The rapist does this to the victim of rape. The child molestor to the child molested. The master to the slave. In each and all such cases, humans who have power exploit those who lack it.

Might the same be true of how humans treat other animals? Undoubtedly there are differences. Anyone who maintains that humans and other animals are the same in all respects is a fool and, as is well and wisely said, only a fool argues with a fool.

But the questions of sameness wears another face. Darwin alludes to this when he notes that the psychological life of the "higher" animals, including those who are raised and slaughtered for food, differs from ours "in degree, not in kind." Granted, these animals do not have all the desires we humans have; granted, they do not comprehend everything we humans comprehend; nevertheless, we and they do have some of the same desires and do comprehend some of the same things.

The desires for food and water, shelter and companionship, freedom of movement and avoidance of pain—these desires are shared by nonhuman animals and human beings. As for comprehension: like humans, many nonhuman animals understand the world in which they live and move. Otherwise, they could not survive.

So beneath the many differences, there is sameness. Like us, these animals embody the mystery and wonder of consciousness. Like us, they are not only in the world, they are aware of it. Like us, they are the psy-

chological centers of a life that is uniquely their own. In these funda-
mental respects humans stand on all fours, so to speak, with hogs and
cows, chickens and turkeys. What these animals are due from us, how
we morally ought to treat them, are questions whose answer begins with
the recognition of our psychological kinship with them.

What happens in slaughterhouses is a variation on the theme of the
exploitation of the weak by the strong. More than ten thousand times
a minute, in excess of six billion times a year, just in the United States,
life is literally drained from so-called food animals. Having the greater
power, humans decide when these animals will die, where they will die,
and how they will die. The interests of these animals themselves play
no role whatsoever in the determination of their fate. Neither does any
law. Lobbyists paid for by the animal agriculture industry have seen to
that. Food animals are explicitly excluded from relevant animal welfare
legislation.

Besides, legislative regulation of slaughter, in the name of protecting nonhuman animals, would be an even greater sham than legislative regulation of meat or plant safety, in the name of protecting human
beings. When, in compliance with current laws, only one percent of
animal carcasses is examined by federal meat inspectors, it is little wonder that millions of Americans daily put themselves and their families
at risk of serious illness, even death, when they eat the contaminated
flesh of sick animals. And when, in 1991, despite various worker-safety
laws, twenty-five poorly paid, nonunionized workers at a Hamlet, North
Carolina poultry processing plant burned to death in a flash fire, because
exit doors were locked (the owner wanted to make sure his workers did
not steal his chickens), the false reassurance of "federal regulation" is
fatally evident. With so little regard for the safety of humans in the packinghouse and for the health of humans at the dinner table, the very idea
of "animal welfare regulations" at the slaughterhouse is, to use Jeremy
Bentham's enduring image, "nonsense upon stilts."

No, the way to end the injustice of slaughter is not through reform
or regulation. Injustice reformed is and always will be justice delayed.

There can be no end to the injustice of slaughter until there is an
end to the business of slaughter. Because corporations that make for-
tunes off the death of hogs, chickens, and other animals will never close
their doors for reasons of conscience, the slaughterhouse walls must be
dissembled, one brick at a time, by acts of conscience performed by one
person at a time. The only way to stop the supply of meat is to elimi-

nate the demand for meat. And the only way to stop the demand for meat is for people to stop eating it. The morally right means to the morally just ends really are that simple.

But the failure of the many to act to eliminate injustice provides no excuse for the few who fail to do so. When it comes to the injustice of human exploitation of other animals for food, it lies within the power of each and every human being to abstain, as a matter of moral principle, from eating meat.

Many people already do. No one can fix the exact number, but it is a good guess that more than half of the world's population, including millions in the United States, Canada, and England, are vegetarians. However large the number, many more would join the growing ranks if they knew the horrors of the slaughterhouse "up close and personal"— saw firsthand the terror in the animal's eyes, the almost liquid descent of the large, surprisingly translucent globs of internal organs spilling from the still breathing, convulsive bodies; watched the methodical skill of the workers as they cut and trim, cut and trim; waded ankle-deep in the rivers of fresh, warm blood; heard the sundering power of chain saws; breathed the fetid odor of life ebbing away. If slaughterhouses had glass walls, would not all of us be vegetarians?

But slaughterhouses do not have glass walls. The architecture of slaughter is opaque, designed in the interests of denial, to ensure that we will not see even if we wanted to look. And who wants to look? It was Emerson who observed, more than a hundred years ago, "You have dined, and however scrupulously the slaughterhouse is concealed in the graceful distance of miles, there is complicity." For an ethic grown lethargic from a happy appetite for ignorance and indulgence, out of sight means out of mind.

Not any more. With the publication of this book, the species genocide practiced in the slaughterhouses of the world is concealed no longer. It is revealed for all to see. And it is revealed in an art noteworthy for what it includes, not for what it omits.

The powerlessness of the animals is here. Uncomprehending and innocent of any wrongdoing, they go to their mechanized, technological death. But no less do we see the tragedies of the workers, their gnarled, twisted bodies molded to their repetitive tasks, their minds drained dull to denial. There is a kind of death that can occur before the body dies. And one thing Sue Coe's stark yet compassionate drawings and paintings show is that not only animals die in slaughterhouses.

But the slaughterhouse is only the final stop for animals raised to be eaten. The enduring images of the idyllic family farm, populated with contented cows grazing in the pasture, free-roaming chickens bustling about the farmyard, hogs wallowing happily in the mud—these bucolic images conceal, they do not reveal today's sordid reality.

That reality is simple. From birth to death, the lives of those animals raised for human consumption are characterized by suffering, deprivation, fear and stress. Every basic interest of these animals is denied. Lack of space. Lack of freedom to move. Lack of companionship. Lack of access to fresh air, sunlight, the very Earth itself. Incredible though it may seem, the vast majority of these animals are raised *permanently indoors*, in densely crowded conditions—living, breathing, but for all intents and purposes inanimate objects, mass-produced on automated "factory farms." For these animals, reduced to so many pounds of flesh sold for so many dollars spent, there is no farmyard, no pasture, no mud. These exist only in the mythology of our imagination.

But there is more. And worse. Roughly herded into the trucks. The frenzied journey to the packinghouse—in the wind and the rain, the snow and the blazing heat. The pandemonium of unloading. The electric prods. The gruesome details of the slaughter. All this, and more— much more—Sue Coe's art places before us, if we will but look, as look we must. No more the excuse, "I didn't know," said even as the trucks roll by, said even as we select from among the body parts entombed in styrofoam containers, said even as we down a Big Mac, gnaw the Colonel's finest, or dine all-so-trendily at Elaine's or Spago.

No, no more excuse, "I didn't know." Sue Coe's art puts an end to that. It is time now to get on with the task of waging the revolution, one person at a time. Isaac Bashevis Singer has his character Herman lament that "for the animals, it is an eternal Treblinka." Let us dare to prove him wrong, one person at a time.

A SHORT, MEAT-ORIENTED HISTORY OF THE WORLD FROM EDEN TO THE MATTOLE

Alexander Cockburn

Start with God.

"And (Peter) saw heaven opened, and a certain vessel descending unto him, as it had been a great sheet knit at the four corners, and let down to the earth: wherein were all manner of fourfooted beasts of the earth, and wild beasts, and creeping things, and fowls of the air. And there came a voice to him, Rise, Peter; kill, and eat." (Acts 10:11-13.)

The Bible is a meat-eater's manifesto. Before the Fall, Adam and Eve were vegetarian. They fed on grains, nuts, and fruits. Then Eve ate the fruit of the tree of knowledge of good and evil (or at least that's the way Adam explained it to God). They were cast forth from the Garden, plunging mankind into original sin from which redemption can come only through the grace of Christ, whose flesh is eaten periodically in the form of the Eucharist. Hardly were Adam and Eve out of Eden before God was offering "respect" to the flesh sacrifice of Abel the keeper of sheep and withholding "respect" from Cain the tiller of the ground. Next thing we know, Cain rose up against his brother Abel, slew him, and we were on our way.[1]

Ringing in Man's ears was the Almighty's edict, as reported in Genesis 1:26-28: "Let us make man in our image, after our likeness: and let them have dominion . . . over all the earth, and over every creeping thing that creepeth upon the earth . . . Be fruitful and multiply, and replenish the earth and subdue it." Thus did the biblical God launch humans on the exploitation of the rest of the natural world, theirs for the using.[2]

Dominion over "Un-Christian" nature was at the heart of it, as C.S. Lewis spelled out frankly enough: "Atheists naturally regard . . . the taming of an animal by man as a purely arbitrary interference of one species with another. The 'real' or 'natural' animal is to them the wild one, and the tame animal is an artificial or unnatural thing. But a Christian must not think so. Man was appointed by God to have dominion over the beasts, and . . . the tame animal is therefore, in the deepest sense, the only 'natural' animal—the only one we see occupying the place it was made to occupy."[3]

Such arrogance towards nonhuman creatures was similarly displayed towards women and human slaves. Not long after His commands in Genesis about animals we find God (in the row immediately following the Fall) telling Eve that "in sorrow shall thou bring forth children; and thy desire shall be to thy husband, and he shall rule over thee."

So far as human slaves were concerned, once again the slave-owners were able to point to Genesis 9, 25-7 and God's curse on Canaan, and the children of Ham: "A servant of servants shall he be unto his brethren." The early Christians never rejected slavery.[4]

Throughout the sixteenth century, intelligent people were having doubts about the distinctiveness of humans or their superior station in the Great Chain of Being. Montaigne wrote that there were no important differences between humans and other animals. The latter, he said, displayed powers of logic, discrimination, judgment, cunning, and even religiosity.[5]

Such sentiments were powerfully abetted by the growing distaste among intellectuals like Erasmus, Sir Thomas More, and Montaigne for hunting, a pursuit whose refinements had transfixed the upper classes for five centuries. "And thus with their butchering and eating of beasts," Erasmus wrote in *In Praise of Folly*, at the start of the sixteenth century, "they (the genteel hunters) accomplish nothing at all unless it be to degenerate into beasts themselves . . . "

Montaigne concluded, "It is apparent that it is not by a true judgement, but by foolish pride and stubbornness, that we set ourselves before the other animals and sequester ourselves from their condition and society."[6]

Sir Thomas More's *Utopia,* published in 1516, brings together some of these themes: "Outside the city are designated places where all gore and offal may be washed away in running water. From these places they transport the carcasses of the animals slaughtered and cleaned by the hands of slaves. They do not allow their citizens to accustom themselves to the butchering of animals, by the practice of which they think that mercy, the finest feeling of our human nature, is gradually killed off."

A few pages further on, More's Utopians "have imposed the whole activity of hunting, as unworthy of free men, upon their butchers—a craft, as I explained before, they exercise through their slaves." There was a long-running popular myth that butchers were, at various periods, excluded from English juries, on the grounds that their trade had coarsened their powers of moral discrimination.[7]

From these humane sentiments of the sixteenth century, we approach the seventeenth century and Descartes, who regarded humans as machinery imbued with the divinely bestowed intellectual essence. Animals were mere machinery. At Port-Royal the Cartesians cut up living creatures with fervor and, in the words of one of Descartes' biographers, "kicked about their dogs and dissected their cats without mercy, laughing at any compassion for them and calling their screams the noise of breaking machinery."

The butchering industry has always been stoutly Cartesian in outlook for obvious reasons. "The breeding sow," an executive from Wall's Meat Co. wrote in *National Hog Farmer* in the late 1970s, "should be thought of, and treated as, a valuable piece of machinery whose function is to pump out baby pigs like a sausage machine."[8]

As a Christian you either concluded with Descartes that animals did not suffer, that their cries were of no greater consequence than the snap of a clock spring breaking, or you reckoned God had a deeper plan, hard for humans to comprehend. John Wesley, the eighteenth-century Methodist divine, thought that animal suffering offered "a plausible objection against the justice of God, in suffering numberless creatures that had never sinned to be so severely punished." Wesley's answer was a sort of Pythagorean metempsychosis, whereby at the last trump they would be resurrected with human intelligence and, thus equipped, enjoy life everlasting.[9]

But the core text for Christians remained the edict in Genesis, along with the divine injunction to St. Peter to kill and eat with God's blessing. St. Francis of Assisi may have had strong rapport with the birds of the air, but in the New World the Franciscans, Jesuits, and Dominicans pioneered cattle ranching.[10]

In 1638 the Jesuits abandoned a mission east of the Rio Plata in what is now Uruguay, leaving behind 5,000 head of cattle. These and other herds multiplied at a staggering rate. By 1700 Felix de Azara reckoned the cattle in what are now Argentina, Uruguay, and Paraguay at 48 million, most of them feral.[11]

Further north these religious orders founded ranches on Marajo, the island in the mouth of the Amazon, in Sonora, in Texas, and in Alta California. By the early nineteenth century, the mission herds in Alta California were estimated at anywhere from 200,000 to 400,000 longhorns of Spanish descent, parents of the gigantic herds later driven to the Inferno of the Chicago stockyards.[12]

Christians have no dietary sanction against eating the flesh of creatures other than themselves. The many days—most notably Fridays in the old Roman Catholic calendar—of nonflesh consumption, were penitential in function. Lent was similar. Contrary to common belief, Hindus do not have a religious interdict on the eating of meat. As in More's *Utopia*, the attitude is caste-based, with Brahmins (intellectuals and priests) and Vaisyas (merchants) regarding meat-eating as the province of Kshatriyas (warriors) and Sudras (laborers). Tanning and butchering are done by the Untouchables. Meat-eating is regarded by Brahmins as unclean, and caste mobility in Hindu society is often expressed by giving up meat and becoming vegetarian.

Many modern Christians don't care much for the prescriptions in Genesis and use the same sort of language one Bishop of Durham once did about the Resurrection: it was all a lot of bother about a heap of old bones. (God responded by striking Durham Cathedral with a lightning bolt, which destroyed it, serving the bishop right.) But the theology still has strength. In an influential essay published in 1967, "The Roots of Our Ecologic Crisis," Lynn White Jr. discussed the verses from Genesis 1: 26-28 about man's dominion over the earth and concluded that "we shall continue to have a worsening ecologic crisis until we reject the Christian axiom that nature has no reason for existence save to serve man."

Thus was the gauntlet thrown down. In 1991, I heard it being picked up by U.S. Representative Bill Dannemeyer, talking to a crowd of businessmen in the Eureka Inn, in Eureka, northern California, not far from where I live. "We should understand," Dannemeyer told the crowd, "that this environmental party has in its objective a mission to change this society, to worship the creation instead of the creator. You have to understand their theology. I can't prove this by empirical analysis, but my gut reaction to their thoughts is simply this: if you go through life and you don't believe in a hereafter and all you see before you today are trees, birds . . . if anybody begins to consume those things, you can get excited about that because it's your whole world. And this is where the militancy comes."

Five years later, at a gun rally outside Detroit, I heard similar execration heaped on environmentalists for preferring rats to humans, plus a savage attack on Jeremy Bentham, the eighteenth-century English utilitarian who famously declared in his *Introduction to Principles of Morals and Legislation*, published in 1780, that animals have rights and that "the question is not, Can they *reason*? nor Can they *talk*? but, Can they *suffer*?"

Bentham drew explicit comparisons between the rights of animals and the rights of slaves, equating the abolitionist cause for human slaves with the cause of rights for animals. Alluding to the French *Code Noir* of 1685, regulating the status of slaves in the West Indies and forbidding their murder by their masters, Bentham expressed the hope that animals would also thus be saved from their torturers and that one day "the number of legs, the villosity of the skin, or the termination of the *os sacrum*" would be equally insufficient reasons for maltreatment.

Soon after the Second World War, Bertrand Russell wrote, "If men developed by such slow stages that there were creatures which we should not know whether to classify as human or not, the question arises: at what stage in evolution did men, or their semi-human ancestors, begin to be all equal? . . . An adherent of evolution may maintain that not only the doctrine of the equality of all men, but also that of the rights of man, must be condemned as unbiological, since it makes too emphatic a distinction between men and other animals."[13]

In his marvelous book on hunting, *A View to a Death in the Morning*, Matt Cartmill quotes Russell on the "too emphatic distinction between men and other animals" and then offers this farewell to the stipulations of the God of Genesis:

> Our culture offers to justify that [too emphatic] distinction by viewing human beings as separate from nature and innately superior to it. At the same time, however, we view the natural order as sacred and establish elaborate machineries to protect it from human intervention. Though different subcultures place different stress on these two views, probably most of us would assent in some degree to both. But it is obvious they do not fit very well together. Our vision of nature as man's holy slave is both incoherent and dishonest, like the patriarchal Victorian vision of Woman as a sort of angelic chattel.
>
> The incoherence and dishonesty inherent in that Victorian ideology were eventually corrected by recognizing that the similarities between master and chattel had greater moral and political importance than the differences. Since there proved to be no morally interesting differences between women and men, the only way men could preserve their self-respect and integrity was to extend citizenship to women. The same was true of masters and slaves and of whites and blacks. In each of these cases, a heavily marked status boundary ultimately had to be given up because it was intellectually indefensible. And if the cognitive boundary between man and beast, between the world of his-

tory and the world of nature, is equally indefensible, we cannot defend human dignity without extending some sort of citizenship to the rest of nature—which means ceasing to treat the non-human world as a series of means to human ends.

Start with God. Now continue with Empire.

In a three-week period in May of 1806, as Lewis and Clark moved through Montana in the course of their survey, they and their party—the Corps of Discovery—killed 167 animals, about eight a day. Reviewing their entire itinerary Donald Worster reckons that over twenty-eight months they probably shot—for needs as opposed to random slaughter—"something between five and ten thousand."[14]

But there was plenty of random slaughter as well. They killed grizzlies, mountain lions, wolves, bobcats, marmots, and of course buffalo. They could pick and choose because the western plains displayed a richness of animal life that overwhelmed many travelers.

Writing a decade into the twentieth century, when this richness had all but gone, the nature writer Ernest Thompson Seton reckoned that near the end of the eighteenth century the "primitive" population of buffalo had been 75 million. By 1895 there were 800 buffalo left, mostly within the borders of Yellowstone Park. Grizzlies, through the mountain and western states, Canada, and Alaska had, in the earlier period, amounted to some 2 million on Seton's estimation. By 1908 they had dwindled to 200,000, almost entirely in Alaska and Canada. Seton reckoned there were maybe 800 in the Lower 48, again mostly around Yellowstone. In mid-1995 there were still about 800 in the Lower 48, though the Fish and Wildlife Service was planning to pull the grizzly off the endangered species list after twenty years, under the pretense that *Ursus horribilis* was no longer imperiled. Translation: Without the pesky bear inhibiting industrial and extractive activities, mining, oil, and timber companies can get on with the business of drilling and chopping, just as God intended for them to do.[15]

On Seton's calculations, elk had dropped from 10 million to 70,000 by 1919. Mule deer did best, with 500,000 left by the time Seton was writing. (He may have exaggerated the original numbers. One later reckoning had the number of buffalo on the continent in 1830 as 40 million. But the variety and number of species lost were still immense.)

By the mid-1870s the buffalo was nearly gone. Colonel Richard Dodge, himself a keen hunter, reckoned that hunters killed over 4 million in the mid-1870s alone: "Where there were myriads of buffalo . . . there were now myriads of carcasses. The air was foul with sickening stench and the vast plain . . . was a dead, solitary, putrid desert." The plains, mountains, valleys profuse with creatures but half a century before were now empty in what one traveler along the South Platte called "the uniformity of its cheerless scenery." Barry Lopez has written of the Great Plains, "If you count the buffalo for hides and the antelope for backstraps and the passenger pigeons for target practice and the Indian ponies (killed by whites, to keep the Indian poor), it is conceivable that 500 million creatures died."[16]

And with these creatures went the Indians' food and way of life. Plenty-Coups, chief of the Crow in Montana, had a dream when he was ten that the white man came with his cattle and destroyed the natural life of the plains. He was right: "When the buffalo went away, we became a changed people. . . . The buffalo was everything to us." Three centuries earlier, the First Viceroy of New Spain had written to his king: "May your lordship realise that if cattle are allowed, the Indians are destroyed."

The buffalo went; Indian time ended. The only place to get food was on the reservations, courtesy of the Indian agent. For a while the Indians made a few dollars gathering up the buffalo bones, shipping off the skeletons, a year or two after the hides. In the buffalos' stead came the white men's cattle.

They came up from Mexico, west through the Appalachians or from the Florida panhandle. In 1850, with the exception of coastal California and east Texas, there was barely a cow or a steer west of the Mississippi. There were more cattle—nearly a million—in New York State than anywhere else. In the whole of the United States the number of cattle (excluding milk cows) added up to almost 11.5 million. By 1870 the total was up to 15 million and by 1900 that had more than doubled again, to 35 million. Texas alone had 6.5 million, and Kansas, Iowa, and Oklahoma had some 2.5 million each on the range or in feedlots.[17] In that half century, industrial meat-eating came of age.

From the fourteenth and fifteenth centuries—when reliable records began to be kept—to the mid-nineteenth century, the European diet varied little. Grains took up about 90 percent of a family's food budget: rye, buckwheat, oats, barley, maize.[18] From the moments that the victuallers and provisioners in the Napoleonic wars pioneered the organization of the mass production line and also modern methods of food preservation, the stage was set for the annihilation of both time and space in matters of food consumption. The vast cattle herds that began to graze the pastures of the western United States, Australia, and Argentina signaled the change.

The speed with which the rhythms and sensibilities of a preindustrial time were abandoned may be judged by descriptions of Haussmann's famous La Villette abattoir, modeled on the old 1807 design approved by Napoleon, and by accounts, virtually contemporaneous of the Union Stockyards in Chicago. La Villette was opened in 1867. Sigfried Giedion describes it in *Mechanization Takes Command*:

> The whole installation bears witness to the care with which the individual animal was treated. The great *lairages* (*bergeries*), with their lofts under the high roofs and their careful design, might have stood in a farmyard; each ox had a stall to itself. . . . In this curious symbiosis of handicraft with centralization lies the peculiarity of this establishment. . . . each ox had a separate booth in which it was felled. This is a survival of handicraft practices, to which the routine of mass slaughtering is unknown. The long houses in which the cattle were slaughtered consisted of rows of single cabins set side by side. Long since, technical installations and slaughtering in large halls have superseded them. It may well be that this treatment in separate booths expresses the deeply rooted experience that the beasts can be raised only at the cost of constant care and attention to the individual animal. The Great Plains beyond the Mississippi, where free tracts of grassland can be dominated from horseback and where the herds grow up almost without care, are implicitly related to the assembly line. In just the same way the peasant farm, where each cow has its name and has to be attended when giving birth to its calf, is linked to handicraft methods in slaughtering.[19]

Giedion's omission here is the feedlot, where the midwestern farmers were able to take the two-year-old "stockers" from the range, then convert their corn into the weight that the "feeders" swiftly put on, before being dispatched on the final stage of their journey through life.

By 1850 the slaughterhouses of Cincinnati—Porkopolis—had been refining the continuous production line for over twenty years. Frederick Law Olmsted, the landscape and park designer, visited Cincinnati in the 1850s.

> We entered an immense low-ceilinged room and followed a vista of dead swine upon their backs, their paws stretching mutely towards heaven. Walking down to the vanishing point we found there a sort of human chopping machine where the hogs were converted into commercial pork. A plank table, two men to lift

and turn, two to wield the cleavers, were its component parts. No iron cog-wheels could work with more regular motion. Plump falls the hog upon the table, chop, chop; chop, chop; chop, chop, fall the cleavers. All is over. But before you can say so, plump, chop, chop; chop, chop; chop, chop, sound again. There is no pause for admiration. By a skilled sleight-of-hand, hams, shoulders, clear, mess, and prime fly off, each squarely cut to its own place, where attendants, aided by trucks and dumb-waiters, dispatch each to its separate destiny—the ham for Mexico, its loin for Bordeaux. Amazed beyond all expectation at the celerity, we took out our watches and counted thirty-five seconds, from the moment when one hog touched the table until the next occupied its place. The numbers of blows required I regret we did not count.[20]

But Cincinnati's hog butchers at that time were not as organized as their successors in the Union yards in Chicago. Much of the hog—head, neck-pieces, backbones—was thrown into the Ohio River.[21]

Many a nineteenth-century traveler stopped in Cincinnati or, later, Chicago to marvel at the efficiency and heartlessness of this unending, furious dispatch of animals to feed New York, Boston, Paris, London, and the increasing industrial armies, and military armies too, that desired to eat meat.

In these years between 1807 and 1865—the opening of the Union Stockyards in Chicago—was perfected the production-line slaughter of living creatures, for the first time in the history of the world. At one end of the trail lay the prairies, the open range, the boisterous pastoral of the cattle drive, where the cowboys sometimes spared a longhorn: "Reed Anthony, Andy Adams' cowman, tells how he and other Confederate soldiers guarding a herd of Texas steers saved the life of one because he would always walk out and stand attentive to the notes of 'Rock of Ages' sung by his herders."[22]

Spared were two or three or ten or a hundred or a thousand from among the millions and millions of creatures that plodded to railheads like Abilene, and thence eastward, or to abattoirs nearer at hand and then bought up by government agents to be sent to the reservations to feed Indians who no longer had buffalo to hunt. As William Cronon writes in *Nature's Metropolis*, in his chapter about Chicago's stockyards:

Cows and cowboys might be symbols of a rugged natural life on the western range, but beef and pork were commodities of the city. Formerly a person could not easily have forgotten that pork and beef were an intricate, symbiotic partnership between animals and human beings. One was not likely to forget that pigs and cattle had died so that people might eat, for one saw them grazing in familiar pastures, and regularly visited the barnyards and butcher shops where they gave up their lives in the service of one's daily meal. In a world of farms and small towns, the ties between field, pasture, butcher shop, and dinner table were everywhere apparent, constant reminders of the relationships that sustained one's own life. In a world of ranches, packing plants, and refrigerator cars, most such connections vanished from easy view.

Cronon emphasizes the consequences of this distancing from killing and commodification of meat: "In the packers' world, it was easy not to remember that eating was a moral act inextricably bound to killing. Such was the second nature that a corporate order had imposed on the American landscape. Forgetfulness was among the least noticed and most important of its by-products."

A later description of the packing plants of Chicago came in Upton Sinclair's 1905 novel, *The Jungle*. His hero, Jurgis, watches pigs being slaughtered: "And yet somehow the most matter-of-fact person could not help thinking of the hogs; they were so innocent, they came so very trustingly; and they were so very human in their protests—and so perfectly within their rights! . . . Now and then a visitor wept, to be sure; but this slaughtering machine ran on, visitors or no visitors. It was like some horrible crime committed in a dungeon, all unseen and unheeded, buried out of sight and memory. One could not stand and watch very long without becoming philosophical, without beginning to deal in symbols and similes, and to hear the hogsqueal of the universe."

Animal slaughter thus became systematized, wrenched from previous bonds of space and time. In Cronon's words, "Geography no longer mattered very much except as a problem in management; time had conspired with capital to annihilate space. The hogs might graze amid forgotten buffalo wallows in central Montana, and the hogs might devour their feedlot corn in Iowa, but from the corporate point of view they might have been anywhere else. Abstract, standardized and fungible, their lives were governed as much by the nature of capital as the nature which gave them life."

The vegetarians and Hitler now enter the story.

With the surge in meat-eating associated with industrial capitalism came—particularly from city-dwellers—a swelling of the vegetarian cause, hitherto confined to a relatively few Pythagoreans, radicals, and eccentrics. Compassion for animals also surged, particularly in Britain where Queen Victoria lent her name to the issue and where antivivisection movements drew increasing adherents, as they did in Germany and France.[23]

The ideological groundwork had been prepared as early as the first century A.D. with Seneca, and the third century, in the writings of the Neoplatonist Porphyry. By the seventeenth century there were vociferous advocates of the view that consumption of animal flesh was aesthetically repulsive, productive of spiritual grossness, and unhealthy besides. (Even earlier, Shakespeare caused Thersites to deride Ajax as "thou mongrel beef-witted lord.") In the seventeenth century Thomas Tryon rejected flesh-eating in part because he was against "killing and oppressing his fellow creatures," in part because flesh gave man "a wolfish, doggist nature." (Both Shakespeare and Tryon were themselves being doggist here, in modern usage.) When Adam and Eve began to eat their fellow creatures after expulsion from Eden, quarreling and war among humanity began. Tryon was also against slavery, ill-treatment of the insane, and discrimination against left-handed people.

The eighteenth century continued to produce an array of arguments in favor of vegetarianism. Scientists argued that man was not made to be carnivorous, given the arrangement of teeth and intestines. Moralists continued to invoke the violence done by animal slaughter to the traits of benevolence and compassion. Butchers were the subject of rebuke, as the poet John Gay urged pedestrians

> To shun the surly butcher's greasy tray,
> Butchers, whose hands are dy'd with blood's foul stain,
> And always foremost in the hangman's train.

British Royal Commissioners a century later found those who worked in abattoirs to be a particularly demoralized trade. The historian Keith Thomas remarks that in the 1790s vegetarianism had radical, even millennial overtones. John Oswald was a radical Scotsman who acquired the vegetarian habit from Hindus while serving in a Highland regiment in India. He wrote *The Cry of Nature* and died fighting for the Jacobins against the Chouans in the Vendée. In Salford, the Bible Christians were founded by William Cowherd as a breakaway sect from the Swedenborgians. Vegetarianism was a condition of entry, and 300 members mustered in support of health, gnosticism, and the tempered life. Cowherd's disciple William Metcalfe led a group of Bible Christians to Philadelphia, where Metcalfe converted Sylvester Graham in 1830, who became a renowned advocate of temperance, vegetarianism, and unbolted flour, and who drew on work by the London doctor William Lamb. The latter's patient John Frank Newton wrote *The Return to Nature*, which much influenced the poet Shelley's 1812 book, *Vindication of Natural Diet*.[24]

But it would be cowardly to accentuate the utopian timbre to much vegetarian thought without also considering the association of vegetarian habit and of solicitude for animals with the Nazis. In April 1933, soon after they had come to power, the Nazis passed laws regulating the slaughter of animals. Later that year Herman Goering announced an end to the "unbearable torture and suffering in animal experiments" and—in an extremely unusual admission of the existence of such institutions—threatened to "commit to concentration camps those who still think they can continue to treat animals as inanimate property." Bans on vivisection were issued—though later partly rescinded—in Bavaria and Prussia. Horses, cats, and apes were singled out for special protection. In 1936 a special law was passed regarding the correct way of dispatching lobsters and crabs and thus mitigating their terminal agonies. Crustaceans were to be thrown into rapidly boiling water. Bureaucrats at the Nazi Ministry of the Interior had produced learned research papers on the kindest method of killing.[25]

Laws protecting wildlife were also passed, under somewhat eugenic protocols: "The duty of a true hunter is not only to hunt but also to nurture and protect wild animals in order that a more varied, stronger and healthier breed shall emerge and be preserved." The Nazis were much concerned about endangered species, and Goering set up nature reserves to protect elk, bison, bears, and wild horses. (Goering called forests "God's cathedrals," thus echoing the idiom of John Muir, one of the fathers of the American national park movement and a despiser of Indians.) The aim of the Law for the Protection of Animals was—as the preamble stated—"to awaken and strengthen compassion as one of the highest moral values of the German people." Animals were to be protected for their own sake rather than as appendages to the human moral and material condition. This was hailed as a new moral concept. In 1934 an international conference in Berlin on the topic of animal protection saw the podium festooned with swastikas and crowned by a banner declaring, "Entire epochs of love will be needed to repay animals for their value and service."

Nazi leaders were noted for love of their pets and for certain animals, notably apex predators like the wolf and the lion. Hitler, a vegetarian and hater of hunting, adored dogs and spent some of his final hours in the company of Blondi, whom he would take for walks outside the bunker at some danger to himself. He had a particular enthusiasm for birds and most of all for wolves. His cover name was Herr Wolf. Many of his interim headquarters had "Wolf" as a prefix, as in Wolfschanze in East Prussia, of which Hitler said "I am the wolf and this is my den." He also liked to whistle the tune of "Who's Afraid of the Big Bad Wolf" from Walt Disney's movie of the Depression, about the Three Little Pigs.

Goebbels said, famously, "The only real friend one has in the end is the dog. . . . The more I get to know the human species, the more I care for my Benno." Goebbels also agreed with Hitler that "meat eating is a perversion in our human nature," and that Christianity was a "symptom of decay," since it did not urge vegetarianism. Rudolf Hess was another affectionate pet owner.

On the one hand, monsters of cruelty towards their fellow humans; on the other, kind to animals and zealous in their interest. In a very fine essay on such contradictions, Arnold Arluke and Boria Sax offer three observations. One, as just noted, many Nazi leaders harbored affection towards animals but antipathy to humans. A maharaja gave Hitler films that displayed animals killing people. The Fuehrer watched with equanimity. Another film showed humans killing animals. Hitler covered his eyes and begged to be told when the slaughter was over. In the same diary passage from the 1920s quoted above, Goebbels wrote, "As soon as I am with a person for three days, I don't like him any longer. . . . I have learned to despise the human being from the bottom of my soul."

Second, animal protection measures "may have been a legal veil to level an attack on the Jews. In making this attack, the Nazis allied themselves with animals since both were portrayed as victims of 'oppressors' such as Jews."

Central to this equation was the composer Richard Wagner, an ardent vegetarian who urged attacks on laboratories and physical assault on vivisectionists, whom he associated with Jews (presumably because of kosher killing methods). Identifying vivisectors as the enemy, Wagner wrote that vivisection of frogs was "the curse of our civilization." Those who failed to untruss and liberate frogs were "enemies of the state."

Vivisection, in Wagner's view, stood for mechanistic science, extrusion of a rationalist intellectualism that assailed the unity of nature, of which man is a part. He believed the purity of Aryans had been compromised by meat-eating and mixing of the races. A nonmeat diet plus the Eucharist would engender a return to the original uncorrupted state of affairs. Wagner borrowed from the Viennese monk, Adolf Lanze, who held that in the beginning there were Aryans and apes, with Germans closest to the former and Jews to the latter. The core enterprise was to perfect the breed and purge the coarser element. This went for animals too, in an unremitting process of genetic purification.

Finally, as Arluke and Sax put it, "the Nazis abolished moral distinctions between animals and people by viewing people as animals. The result was that animals could be considered 'higher' than some people."

The blond Aryan beast of Nietzsche represented animality at the highest available grade, at one with wild nature. But spirituality could be associated with animals destined for the table, as in this piece of German farm propaganda: "The Nordic peoples accord the pig the highest possible honor . . . in the cult of the Germans the pig occupies the first place and is the first among the domestic animals. . . . The predominance of the pig, the sacred animal destined to sacrifices among the Nordic peoples, has drawn its originality from the great trees of the German forest. The Semites do not understand the pig, they reject the pig, whereas this animal occupies the first place in the cult of the Nordic people."

Aryans and animals were allied in a struggle against the contaminators, the vivisectors, the undercreatures. "The Fuehrer," Goebbels wrote "is deeply religious, though completely anti-Christian. He views Christianity as a symptom of decay. Rightly so. It is a branch of the Jewish race. . . . Both [Judaism and Christianity] have no point of contact to the animal element, and thus, in the end they will be destroyed. The Fuehrer is a convinced vegetarian on principle."

Race purification was often seen in terms of farm improvement, eliminating poor stock, and improving the herd. Martin Bormann had been an agricultural student and manager of a large farm. Himmler had been a chicken breeder. Medical researchers in the Third Reich, Arluke and Sax write, "also approached Germans as livestock. For instance, those familiar with Mengele's concentration camp experiments believed that his thoughtlessness about the suffering of his victims stemmed from his passion about creating a genetically pure super-race, as though you were breeding horses." Those contaminating Aryan stock were "lower animals" and should be dispatched. Seeing such people as low and coarse animal forms allowed their production-line slaughter. Hoss, the Auschwitz commandant, was a great lover of animals, particularly horses, and after a hard day's work in the death camp liked to stroll about the stables.

"Nazi German identity," Arluke and Sax conclude, "relied on the blurring of boundaries between humans and animals and the constructing of a unique phylogenetic hierarchy that altered conventional human-animal distinctions and imperatives. . . . As part of the natural order, Germans of Aryan stock were to be bred like farm stock, while 'lower animals' or 'subhumans,' such as the Jews and other victims of the Holocaust were to be exterminated like vermin as testament to the new 'natural' and biological order conceived under the Third Reich."

Animal rights advocates and vegetarians often fidget under jeers that it was Nazis who banned vivisection. In fact vivisection continued through the Third Reich. The British journal *The Lancet* commented on the Nazis' animal experimentation laws of 1933 that "it will be seen from the text of these regulations that those restrictions imposed [in Germany] follow rather closely those enforced in [England]."

The moral is not that there is something inherently Nazi-like in campaigning against vivisection or deploring the eating of animal meat or reviling the cruelties of the feedlot and the abattoir. The moral is that ideologies of nature imbued with corrupt race theory and a degraded romanticism can lead people up the wrong path, one whose terminus was an abattoir for "unhealthy" humans, constructed as a reverse image of the death camp for (supposedly) healthy animals to be consumed by humans. For the Nazis their death camps were, in a way, romanticism's revenge for the abattoirs and the hogsqueal of the universe as echoing from the Union Stockyards in Chicago.

"Earth felt the wound," wrote Milton of the Fall.

Intensive meat production—these days mostly of beef, veal, pork, and chicken—is an act of violence: primarily, of course, an act of violence against the creatures involved. But it is also violence against nature and against poor people.

Soon after the Spanish conquerors overwhelmed the Aztec capital of Tenochtitlán in 1521, the colonist-pastoralists began to take over agricultural lands for sheep and cattle. Among such lands was what later became named the Valle de Mezquital, in highland central Mexico, centered on the Tula and Moctezuma river drainages in what is now the state of Hidalgo. In the early sixteenth century, this Valle de Mezquital was the site of intensive irrigation agriculture by the Otomí Indians, with such crops as maize, chiles, maguey, nopal, squash, and beans. The soils were good and vegetative cover on the hills rich enough to catch the sparse rainwater and keep the water table high enough to feed the springs and irrigation systems. There were forests of oak and pine.[26]

Old World grazing animals entered the Valle in the late 1520s, in the form of cattle, horses, pigs, and goats. By the 1540s there were forty-one flocks of sheep of around a thousand head each. With them came African slaves as their shepherds. Soon Indians were complaining about damage done by the alien stock to their lands and crops. The Spanish governor banned cattle and horses from the densely populated central regions, but with the competition for forage thus diminished, the sheep population erupted. By 1565 there were 2 million sheep in the Valle.

Meanwhile the Otomí were dying. Through the century, the population fell by as much as 90 percent. The Great Cocoliste epidemic of 1576-81 was the coup de grâce. Sheep began to take over from people, as the Spanish increased their stocking rates to as much as 20,000 head of sheep per station.

This profusion of animals rapidly changed the terrain. Vegetation diminished and often only bare soil remained. Fields went to pasture. Forests were chopped down for more pasture, also for use in the Spanish mines. During the last quarter of the century, semiarid species such as mesquite, cardon, yucca, thorn scrub, and lechuguilla maguey started to take over. The fallow lands of the decimated Indians and the pastures of the colonists were now covered in mesquite bush and thistles. With less and less to eat, the sheep population dropped sharply. The weight of sheep killed for meat dropped too.

"By 1600," Elinor Melville writes in her excellent account of these ecological consequences of pastoral colonization, "sheet erosion scarred the hillsides and covered the flat and sloping lands with slope-wash debris. In a final blow to irrigation agriculture, springs were dying out in many parts of the region. By the end of the sixteenth century the landscape was the eroded and gullied mesquite desert traditionally associated with the Valle de Mezquital."

One hundred years later the Valle finally received its modern name—"the place where mesquite grows"—and became the Mexican symbol for arid poverty, a symbolism it retains even though today the region receives Mexico City's effluent, which renders it the site of intensive agriculture. Those who do not know the history ascribe its present fertility to modern technology and the sewage of Mexico City. But, as Melville says, it is not an indigenous landscape, it is a conquest landscape.

David Hamilton Wright, a biologist at the University of Georgia, once wrote that "an alien ecologist observing . . . earth might conclude that cattle is the dominant species in our biosphere."[27] The modern livestock economy and the passion for meat have radically altered the look of the planet. Today, across huge swaths of the globe, from Australia to the western plains of the United States, one sees the conquest landscapes of the European mass-meat-producers and their herds of ungulates. Because of romantic ideas of "unchanging" landscapes it is hard to grasp the rapidity of this process, with spans as short as thirty-five years between the irruption of a herd onto virgin terrain, overgrazing, soil erosion, crash, and eventual stabilization, with the plant communities finally leveling out, though reduced in richness and variety, and the land altered forever.

By 1795, nearly 112,000 cattle were grazing the ranges of Tamaulipas, along the Mexican Gulf coast. These herds—plus no less than 130,000 horses—inflicted major environmental damage on the native grasses. The grasslands began to give way to thornbushes. By the 1930s the pastures had been so overgrazed and degraded that forty acres were required for each cow.[28]

Starting around 1825 these Spanish cattle, along with herds coming from the east, through Louisiana, formed the basis of the Texas ranching system, which took the following half century to collapse, wiped out by ecological maladaptation, otherwise known as cold and drought. By the 1880s, in the words of Terry Jordan, free grass outside of Oklahoma "greatly encouraged overstocking, as did a serious misreading of the pastoral capacity of the fragile short-grass plains and the speculation-fueled, hypercommercialized cattle boom of the early 1880s. The resulting cattle glut both severely damaged the ranges and, by 1886, led to a crash in beef prices. Livestock dumped on the market because the depleted pastures could no longer support them further depressed prices. Even so, thousands of additional cattle died due to the deteriorated condition of the ranges." The terrible winters of 1886 and 1887—the worst in recorded memory—finished off the boom. Millions of cattle died, and the pastures were savagely degraded. Across the years the cattle grazed on the tall grasses—big and little bluestem—particularly where ranchers fenced off the water-courses and springs from their competitors. Ironweed and goldenrod invaded, along with Kentucky bluegrass. Short grasses and annual weeds took over.

In the late eighteenth century when the first cattle herds arrived in what the Spanish colonists called Alta California, the region presented itself as a Mediterranean landscape, but of a sort that had been extinguished in Europe for many centuries. There were meadows with perennial bunchgrasses, beardless wild rye, oat grass, perennial forbs: 22 million acres of such prairie and 500,000 acres of marsh grass. Beyond this, there were 8 million acres of live oak woodlands and parklike forests. Beyond and above these, the chaparral.

By the 1860s, in the wake of the gold rush, some 3 million cattle were grazing California's open ranges and the degradation was rapid, particularly as ranchers had been overstocking to cash in on the cattle boom. Floods and drought between 1862 and 1865 consummated the ecological crisis. In the spring of 1863, 97,000 cattle were grazing in parched Santa Barbara County. Two years later only 12,100 remained. By the mid-1860s, in Terry Jordan's words, "many ranges stood virtually denuded of palatable vegetation." In less than a century, California's pastoral utopia had been destroyed; the ranchers moved east of the Sierra Nevada into the Great Basin, or north, to colder and dryer terrain.

These days travelers heading north through California's Central Valley can gaze at mile upon mile of environmental wreckage: arid land except where irrigated by water brought in from the north, absurdly dedicated to producing cotton. Some two hundred miles north of Los Angeles, fierce stench and clouds of dust herald the Harris Beef feedlot. On the east side of the interstate several thousand steers are penned, occasionally doused by water sprays. After a few minutes of this Dantesque spectacle the barren landscape resumes, with one of California's state prisons at Coalinga—unlike the beef feedlot, secluded from view—lying just over the horizon to the west.

California is one of America's largest dairy states, and livestock agriculture uses almost one third of all irrigation water. It takes 360 gallons of water to produce a pound of beef (irrigation for grain, trough-water for stock), which is why, further east in the feedlot states of Colorado, Nebraska, and Kansas; along with the Texas panhandle, the Oglalla aquifer has been so severely depleted. (California's Central Valley itself faces increasing problems of salty water from excessive use of groundwater.)

Deep-drilling for water came as response to the Dustbowl disaster of the 1930s, itself produced by farming ill-adapted to the natural conditions. Intensive pumping of the high plains aquifer began after the Second World War. By 1978 there were 170,000 wells drawing off 23 million acre-feet of water each year. (An acre-foot represents the amount of water required to cover one acre with water one foot deep.) This is what is needed to support a livestock industry worth $10 billion a year, from grain fields to slaughterhouses such as the Holcomb abattoir of the Iowa Beef Co., covering fourteen acres.[29]

The gasoline, diesel fuel, natural gas, and electricity required to pump the water up several hundred feet from the shrinking aquifer are as finite as the water itself. Sometime in the next century the high plains will be forced back to dryland farming, with such descendants of the present population as remain facing other environmental disasters: poisoning of the remaining groundwater by herbicides, fertilizer, and vast amounts of nitrogen and phosphorus from the manure excreted day by day in the feedlots. Some of the latter ends up in the air as gaseous ammonia. At the end of the 1980s, Frank and Deborah Popper of Rutgers University began arguing that an era of agricultural "pullback" lay ahead, and the future of the plains might hold (though later they said that it was more a metaphor than a concrete proposal) a "buffalo commons" in which native animals such as the buffalo would roam over federally owned grass-lands once more.

Unsustainable grazing and ranching sacrifice drylands, forests, and wild species. Brazil's military dictators, who came to power in the early 1960s, hoped to convert their nation's Amazonian rain forests, which cover more than 60 percent of the country, to cattle pasture and thus make Brazil a major beef producer on the world market. A speculative frenzy ensued, with big companies acquiring million-acre spreads that they promptly stripped of trees in order to get tax write-offs and kin-dred subsidies from the junta. Big ranchers, rather than the peasant set-tler-pyromaniacs of song and story, accounted for most of the destruction. Within a decade or so, degraded scrubland had yielded money to the corporations but few cattle, and none of these could be sold on the world market because they were diseased. Indeed the Ama-zon is a net beef-importing region. Meanwhile many of the 2 or 3 mil-lion people who lived in the rain forest have been evicted with each encroachment of the burning season.[30]

Such are the assaults on the environment and on the poor.[31] By 1990 about half of all American rangeland was severely degraded, with habi-tats along narrow streams the worst in memory. Australian pastures show the same pattern. In the drylands of South Africa, overgrazing has made over 7 million acres useless for cattle, and 35 million acres of savanna are rapidly becoming equally useless as overgrazing takes its toll.

Humans are essentially vegetarian as a species and insatiate meat-eating brings its familiar toll of heart disease, stroke, cancer. The enthusiasm for meat also produces its paradox: hunger. A people living on cereals and legumes for protein need to grow far less grain than a people eating creatures that have been fed by cereals. For years Western journalists described in mournful tones the scrawny and costly pieces of meat available in Moscow's shops, associating the lack with backwardness and the failure of communism. But from 1950 meat consumption in the Soviet Union tripled. By 1964 grain for livestock feed outstripped grain for bread and by the time the Soviet Union collapsed, livestock were eating three times as much grain as humans. All of this required greater and greater imports of grain until precious foreign exchange made the Soviet Union the world's second largest grain importer, while a dietary "pattern" based on excellent bread was vanishing.

Governments—prodded by the World Bank—plunged into schemes for intensive grain-based meat production, which favors large, rich producers and penalizes small subsistence farmers. In Mexico the share of cropland growing feed and fodder for animals went from 5 percent in 1960 to 23 percent in 1980. Sorghum, used for animal feed, is now Mexico's second largest crop by area. At the same time, the area of land producing the staples for poor folk in Mexico—corn, rice, wheat, and beans—has fallen relentlessly. Mexico is now a net corn importer, with imports from rich countries such as Canada and the United States wiping out millions of subsistence farmers who have to migrate to the cities or to El Norte. Mexico feeds 30 percent of its grain to livestock—pork and chickens for urban eaters—while 22 percent of the population suffers from malnutrition.

Multiply this baneful pattern across the world. Meanwhile the classic pastoralists who have historically provided most of the meat in Africa with grazing systems closely adapted to varying environments are being marginalized by privatization, closing off of access rights, and plans by governments to shift them to settled farming and prevent their wandering ways. Elsewhere, small farmers are similarly marginalized. Grain-based livestock production inexorably leads to larger and larger units and economies of scale.

Come now to a parable of swine.

Not so many years ago in North Carolina, the pig barons sensed opportunity for their "right to work" state. In the traditional hog belt of the Midwest, unions and laws against some forms of agribusiness still protect the medium-sized farmer. Today, in North Carolina the hog industry is headed the same way chicken production went thirty years ago, with the vertical integration pioneered by Frank Purdue and others wiping out a million small chicken farmers across the country.[32]

The coastal plains and piedmont of North Carolina are now pocked by vast pig factories and pig slaughterhouses. People living here sicken from the stink of twenty-five-foot deep lagoons of pig shit that have poisoned the water table and decanted nitrogen and phosphorous-laced sludge into such rivers as the Neuse, the Tar-Pamlico, and the Albemarle. Ammonia gas burdens the air, just as it does in northern Europe (doing more damage in Holland than factories or cars) where at least open lagoons are banned, and the pig shit must be "injected" into croplands rather than sprayed over them, as is the habit in the United States. In North Carolina it is as though the sewage of 15 million people were being flushed into open pits and sprayed onto fields, with almost no restrictions. That's where 7 million pigs' worth of manure goes.

Small hog producers have been bankrupted or become "contract" producers for the giants, bearing the up-front costs. The economies of scale produce fewer jobs than in the chicken business or in the tobacco industry, which hog raising is increasingly replacing.

To insulate themselves from popular outrage or even regulatory surveillance, the pig barons have either bought political protection or gone directly into politics, where they write or endorse laws favorable to themselves.

Most conspicuous in this art is Wendell Murphy, head of Murphy Farms, the biggest pig business in the country, selling $200 million worth of hogs in 1994. Murphy joined the state legislature in 1982 and soon augmented the steady stream of laws protecting hog and chicken interests. In North Carolina, legislators may make money off the bills or amendments or votes they offer so long as they can assert that such profit possibilities do not cloud their judgment. Presumptively unclouded, Murphy pushed through or supported laws exempting his business from sales taxes, inspection fees, property taxes on feed, zoning laws, and pollution fines. Laws imposing harsh penalties on animal rights activists were also advanced and ratified. In 1993, after Murphy had left the assembly, one of his executives was still there to press successfully for a bill that blocked environmental researchers from getting state agriculture department records on hog farm sites and sizes. In 1991, when Murphy was still installed as tribune for the pig business, the North Carolina legislature brazenly passed Senate Bill 669 allowing the N.C. Pork Producers Association to collect a hog levy, which could be used to lobby state legislators, fight lawsuits, and pursue purposes prohibited with money derived from a federal check-off.

Pork is power in North Carolina. In 1988 when a particularly dear friend of the hog, chicken, and turkey industries—Senator Harold "Bull" Hardison—was running for the Democratic nomination for lieutenant governor in North Carolina, Murphy gave him $100,000. A few days later Hardison got another $100,000 from Marvin Johnson, head of Raeford Farms, one of the biggest turkey processors in the country. The legal maximum in such primary elections is $4,000. The State Bureau of Investigations uncovered these illegal disbursements, but announced in 1993 that given the two-year statute of limitations Murphy and Johnson could not be touched. Hardison had done his part by advancing the laws protecting the pig barons from environmental laws and sales taxes.

The pig men of North Carolina have a friend even higher up the political chain, in the form of U.S. Senator Lauch Faircloth, a Republican who is part owner of Coharie Farms, the thirtieth largest hog producer in the country. Faircloth also owns more than $1 million worth of stock in two slaughterhouses. In Congress he is now ensconced as chairman of the Senate Subcommittee on Clean Water, Wetland, Private Property and Nuclear Safety.

Just as with Don Tyson, Arkansas' chicken king, North Carolina's pig barons have the place sewn up, even without Murphy there as an elected rep. John M. Nichols, the Republican who leads North Carolina's House Committee on Health and Environment, is also a member of its House Agriculture Committee. He is now building a 2,400-sow farm in Craven County that will raise pigs for Murphy. Leo Daughtry, North Carolina's House majority leader, owns a part interest in Johnson County Hams, which cures about 60,000 hams a year. Murphy's old seat is now occupied by Charles Albertson, a country music singer and former employee of the U.S. Department of Agriculture, who won his seat with the help of pork money. After two terms in the North Carolina House he rose to the senatorial purple in 1993, where he was named chairman of the Agriculture, Marine Resources and Wildlife Committee.

Such is the swollen empire of pork in North Carolina. Its reeking lagoons surround darkened warehouses of animals trapped in metal crates barely larger than their bodies, tails chopped off, pumped with corn, soybeans, and chemicals until, in six months, they weigh about 240 pounds, at which point they are shipped off to abattoirs to be killed, sometimes by prisoners on work release from the county jail. Near the town of Tar Heel, in Smithfield's Carolina Foods abattoir, half the workforce are Latin American immigrants; a number of others are prisoners. The sows are killed after about two years or whenever their reproductive performance declines. It takes maybe eight to ten people to run a sow factory, overseeing 2,000 sows, boars, and piglets. A computerized "finishing" farm, where the pigs are fattened, may just require a part-time caretaker to check the equipment and clean up between arriving and departing cohorts of hogs. The noise in these factories is ghastly, and many workers wear ear pads against the squealing and crashing of the animals in their cages. When the *Raleigh News and Observer* did a series on North Carolina's pig barons in early 1995 (following a pioneering article in *Southern Exposure* in 1992), readers were told they could call the paper's number in Raleigh, 549-5100, extension 4647, and listen to a recording of this terrible sound. Thus do we travel toward necropolis from Olmsted's visit to Porkopolis nearly a century and a half ago.

Art met meat early on.

Nearly 20,000 years ago a Paleolithic artist drew an aurochs—or wild ox—in black pigment on the walls of a cave at Lascaux, near what is now called Montignac, in the department of the Dordogne in France. He made the aurochs—ancestor of the Spanish fighting bulls and of the Longhorns—eighteen feet long, its outline first sketched out with bird feathers, then etched in with a stone blade. The artist prepared the surface with fat and oil, then blew powdered ochre onto it through a bone tube.

In the lower gallery at Lascaux there's a picture of a man lying dead. He had evidently been attacked by an aurochs, which itself had a lance in its flank and entrails hanging from its belly. Before the man, on a pole, is a bird. Throughout the cave there are many paintings of pregnant animals.

Art here was surely an instrument of magic, an expression of ritual; magic not contrived in sorrow and repentance, but in hope; art enlisted, in Arnold Hauser's words, "to secure the path to future enjoyment."

The relationships between people and other creatures in the Paleolithic period necessarily remain mysterious. Discussing how hunters and gatherers perceive their environments, Tim Ingold cites one example:

Among the Cree Indians of Northern Canada, it is believed that animals intentionally present themselves to the hunter to be killed. The hunter consumes the meat, but the soul of the animal is released to be reclothed with flesh. Hunting there, as among many northern peoples, is conceived as a rite of regeneration: consumption follows killing as birth follows intercourse, and both acts are integral to the reproductive cycles, respectively, of animals and humans. However, animals will not return to hunters who have treated them badly in the past. One treats an animal badly by failing to observe the proper disposal of the bones, or by causing undue pain and suffering to the animal in killing it. Above all, animals are offended by *unnecessary* killing: that is, by killing as an end in itself rather than to satisfy genuine consumption needs. They are offended, too, if the meat is not properly shared by all those in the community who need it. Thus meat and other usable products should on no account be wasted.[33]

The "path to future enjoyment" was next secured by the domestication of animals, which turns out to be the main topic of the Middle Eastern Holy Books, much of which consist of bragging about the size of herds and flocks. The self-sustaining family farm or the journeys of the pastoralists were well on the path to destruction by the mid-nineteenth century, with the rise of the modern commodity markets. But the values of family-farm life remain an important ingredient of the culture of consumption: not Murphy Hog Industries, but Murphy Farms. Not John's Slaughterhouse, but Farmer Johns in Los Angeles. Hence, restating Hauser, the "needs of everyday life" today require that we use the magic of art to conceal the slaughterhouse. Our "needs" are a continual supply of meat, not provided by the chances of the hunt, nor by the family farm with Peter the Pig and Daisy the Cow, but refrigerated in plastic wrap, dissociated from an animal context and accompanied by the quiet assurance that it can always be obtained by money. The modern cave painter should depict a credit card and a Safeway. But in general, art hasn't made the transition from the preindustrial state, when 90 percent of the world was peasant and 10 percent "other," with the latter living off the surplus of the former. From this world come most of our values and sentiments about the animals we have domesticated for work, companionship, and food.

The British artist Sue Coe, who now lives in New York, escorts us to our modern state. In terms of art history the only previous depictions of this sort were of the Day of Judgment, of Inferno, as for example displayed by Coppo di Marcovaldo in the Baptistry in Florence. Coe gives us the meat machinery of the slaughterhouse depicted as the day of judgment, with no heaven, only the purgatory of the feedlot, and the hell fires of death.

And finally, on a personal note.

I wrote those last words and went forth with my friends Karen and Joe Paff to chop up the carcasses of two sheep on the tailgate of Joe's pick-up outside my house: one for my deep-freeze, the other for the Paffs. Our neighbors, Greg and Margie Smith, had raised the sheep on their fields a couple of miles further down the Mattole River.

Unlike Sue Coe, I'm not a vegetarian. She once sent me a wonderful print of hers called *Modern Man Followed by the Ghosts of His Meat*, a fellow accompanied by an accusatory posse of pigs, chickens, cows, and sheep. The posse after me would be ample enough, starting with the crow my mother trapped during the Blitz in London, continuing with whale (wartime London again), and then picking up with the bullocks I helped consume, raised by local butchers on their farms around the southern Irish town of Youghal where I grew up.

These days I live in Humboldt County, in the Mattole Valley, a couple of hours drive south of Eureka. The ranchers here run cattle on the hills, or the river bottom, or the King Range, which is controlled by the Bureau of Land Management. The sheep have come and mostly gone. Here it's cattle, raised and grazed, and shipped off to the feedlots.

I suppose my house goes through a couple of sheep, a pig, and a hindquarter of a cow each year. The pig would be one raised by a 4-H kid—Cisco Benemann's was the best so far—from around Ferndale, an hour over the hills, and killed and cut up by a local butcher. The cow for the last two years was called Mochie, raised by Michael Evenson.

At a Christmas party last year I ate a good piece of beef, said so, and Michael told me it was from Mochie and sold me a hindquarter. He gave me this little piece of Homeric history about her origins, which go back to the early 1970s, when a number of counterculture folk headed north from the Bay Area and settled in southern Humboldt.

Michael bought Mochie's grandmother as a day-old calf in a Fortuna auction in 1972. She gave good milk in Michael's three-cow dairy. At the age of sixteen or seventeen she'd had fourteen calves and earned retirement. She died in the pasture of natural causes at the age of twenty-two. Her last calf was a heifer, who herself had fourteen calves. Michael sold her to a couple that wanted a milk cow, and he got back the calf she was about to have.

So the animal you had part of was that calf that came to me. I was out of milking and dairy by then. I had very few animals and the pasture was in perfect condition. About sixty acres. When I first got there, we figured about fifteen acres a cow but after we reseeded it, this dropped down to ten. When you reseed, you reseed a balanced diet, with perennial and annual grasses, so the soil is always alive with something. A lot of variety. It was a mix Fred Hurlbutt, a rancher in Garberville, developed. My animals were slaughtered in winter, and the butcher thought they'd been on grain. I don't grain feed animals. Too concentrated and unbalanced. My animals always had choices, in the kind of grasses to eat and where to sleep. I had cross fencing, but they were generous enough pastures and choice. I had goats in the 1960s, and they really taught me animals like choices. They let you know when they're not happy. There have never been any diseases on my place.

Bullocks I'd slaughter after about two years. I don't lie to my animals. I tell them the only way I know, using English, that I'm going to slaughter them. I give them as much love and care as I can. Then, when they're slaughtered they will be part of my body, part of your body. You do the same in your garden.

The couple I sold Mochie's mother to are hippies living east of the Eel River. She's a midwife and he grows lettuce. They're new settlers, and they were the ones who called the calf Mochie. I never sent any animal to a commercial slaughterhouse. Mochie was four and she was breaking fences and wandering. I used a 30.30 and shot her behind the ear, out through the eye.

Michael is off red meat now. A friend of his, the late John Iris, who started the Wild Iris Institute for Sustainable Forestry, got bone cancer when he was fairly young. In the military he'd worked in missile silos in Europe and with nuclear warheads in Vietnam. He lived in Briceland and went on a macrobiotic diet. Michael joined him, eating fish and chicken, but nothing from the nightshade family, for example tomatoes or potatoes. No milk, no red meat, "even though I had a freezer full of beef and a cow I was milking. I felt better. I'm realizing now my life has changed because I no longer have twice daily contact with cows. I wouldn't say life is more peaceful. It became more turbulent."

So much for versions of pastoral in the Mattole Valley. Most people don't have the option of getting Greg Smith to kill them a lamb. Probably most people wouldn't want to cut it up. Someone in the supermarket in Garberville the other day went to the manager and complained because the meat counter man had some bloodstains on his apron. But even so, there are options. If you don't like the thought of debeaked chickens sitting in a wire box all their lives, don't buy them.[34] Fgure out if you can have a meal that squares with ethical standards you can live with, or even vaguely aspire to. If you don't want to eat a piece of an animal tortured by hog barons, then cut up by prisoners, ask yourself, is there a way out (aside from campaigning against such cruelties and conditions) at a level that goes beyond eating the pre-Fall diet only so long as Sue Coe's paintings remain vivid in your mind.

NOTES

1. God's line is that it's Man's and Woman's fault. He set up a vegetarian world and then the founding parents, exercising free will, wrecked everything, and creatures fell to eating one another. "Vegetarianism was also encouraged by Christian teaching, for all theologians agreed that man had not originally been carnivorous. . . . Many biblical commentators maintained that it was only after the flood that humans became meateaters; in the period of disorientation following the Fall they had remained herbivorous. Others, noting that Abel was a herdsman, suggested that it was the Fall which had inaugurated the carnivorous error and that the liberty of eating flesh which God gave Noah was merely the renewal of an earlier permission. Commentators argued as to whether meat-eating had been permitted because man's physical constitution had degenerated and therefore required new forms of nutriment, or because the cultivation of the soil to which he was condemned required a more robust food, or because the fruits and herbs on which he had fed in Eden had lost their former goodness. But everyone agreed that meat-eating symbolised man's fallen condition. 'God allows us to take away the lives of our fellow creatures and to eat their flesh,' wrote Richard Baxter in 1691, 'to show what sin hath brought on the world.' The death of brute animals to supply the wants of sinful man could even be made a paradigm of Christ's atonement." Keith Thomas, *Man and the Natural World* (New York: Pantheon, 1983).

2. Man is "this thing," Francis Bacon wrote in *The Wisdom of the Ancients*, as he proposed his principles of scientific investigation in the early seventeenth century, "in which the whole world centers, with respect to final causes; so that if he were away, all other things would stray and fluctuate, without end or intention, or become perfectly disjointed and out of frame; for all things are made subservient to man, and he receives uses and benefits from them all . . . so that everything in nature seems made not for itself, but for man." In Bacon's view, the Fall had suspended man's sovereignty over nature; and to restore this prelapsarian dominance was the proper aim of all science, whose true aim, as he put it in the *Novum Organum*, is "to extend more widely the limits of the power and greatness of man," and to endow him with "infinite commodities."

   Tyson or Purdue should have Bacon's portrait on every chicken shed. Always alert to the possible utility of nature to man, Bacon was riding along in his coach in the early English spring of 1626, when the notion of experimenting with frozen chicken crossed his mind. He stopped the coach, descended, bought a fowl, and stuffed it with snow, thus contracting the chill from which he soon died in Lord Arundel's house a few weeks later.

   Bacon discusses vivisection in somewhat muffled terms: "To prosecute such inquiry concerning perfect animals by cutting out the foetus from the womb would be too inhuman, except when opportunities are afforded by abortions, the chase, and the like. There should therefore be a sort of nightwatch over nature, as showing herself better by night than by day. For these may be regarded as night studies by reason of the smallness of our candle and its continual burning." *Novum Organum*, Book II, 41.

But while Bacon was indulging himself in these niceties, his doctor, William Harvey (who also looked after Arundel) was busy vivisecting. Bacon published the *Novum Organum* in 1620. Harvey published his treatise on the circulation of the blood, *De Motu Cordis et Sanguinis* in Frankfurt in 1621. It began with the words, "When, by many dissections of living animals, as they came to hand . . . I first gave myself to observing how I might discover . . ." He presumably discussed his work with Bacon, who didn't feel affronted enough to change doctors.

3. C.S. Lewis, *The Problem of Pain* (New York: Macmillan, 1962). Cited in Matt Cartmill, *A View to a Death in the Morning: Hunting and Nature through History* (Cambridge: Harvard University Press,1993). Christian and Marxist shook hands over this deal. Cartmill reports that in the 1930s "some Marxist thinkers . . . urged that it was time to put an end to nature and that animals and plants that serve no human purpose ought to be exterminated."

4. The historian Geoffrey de Ste Croix declared that he was not aware of any general Christian condemnation of slavery before the petition of the Mennonites of Germantown in Pennsylvania in 1688, and the Mennonites were founded by a sixteenth-century Anabaptist, whose attitude to property was communist in outlook. See G.E.M. de Ste Croix, *The Class Struggle in the Ancient Greek World from the Archaic Age to the Arab Conquests* (London: Duckworth, 1981).

5. "Presumption is our natural and original malady. The most vulnerable and frail of all creatures is man, and at the same time the most arrogant. He feels and sees himself lodged here, among the mire and dung of the world, nailed and riveted to the worst, the deadest and most stagnant part of the universe, on the lowest story of the house and the farthest from the vault of heaven, with the animals of the worst condition of the three [i.e. those that walk, fly and swim], and in his imagination he goes planting himself above the circle of the moon, and bringing the sky down beneath his feet. It is by the vanity of this same imagination that he equals himself to God, attributes to himself divine characteristics, picks himself out and separates himself from the horde of other creatures, carves out their shares to his fellows and companions the animals, and distributes among them such portions of faculties and powers as he sees fit. How does he know, by the force of his intelligence, the secret internal stirrings of animals? By what comparison between them and us does he infer the stupidity that he attributes to them?"

Amplifying his essays a few years later Montaigne added after the passage just quoted, the famous sentence "When I play with my cat, who knows if I am not a pastime to her more than she is to me?" From "Apology for Raymond Sebond," *The Complete Essays of Montaigne,* tran. Donald M. Frame (Stanford: Stanford University Press, 1965).

6. By the mid-sixteenth century Giovanni Battista Gelli, a Florentine scholar, was writing *Circe*, a dialogue in which the enchantress of the title tells Ulysses she will restore the animals she transmogrified back into his original crew, so long as he can secure their agreement. The animals remain unpersuaded. You men, the doe replies to Ulysses' invitation to resume the form of a woman, "make mere slaves and servants out of us . . . Among animals, any animals you want to name, the female partakes equally with the male in his pleasures and diversions." Only one, an elephant, makes the return journey and shouts triumphantly, "What a marvelous sensation it is to be a man!" But he was a philosopher. *The Circe of Signior Giovanni Battista Gelli*, ed. R. Adams (Ithaca: Cornell University Press, 1991). Cited in Matt Cartmill, op. cit.

7. Sir Thomas More, *Utopia*, ed. Edward Sturz (New Haven: Yale University Press, 1964). Discussion of the legend of jury exclusion of butchers in Keith Thomas, op. cit.

8. Jim Mason and Peter Singer, *Animal Factories* (New York: Harmony, 1990).

9. Cartmill, op. cit. This concept of eighteenth-century promotion was resumed by a French biologist, Charles Bonnet, who thought that man would eventually move on "to another dwelling place, more suitable to the superiority of his faculties," and then the beasts would be elevated accordingly: "In this universal restoration of animals, there

may be found a Leibniz or a Newton among the monkeys or the elephants, a Perrault or a Vauban among the beavers."

10. Christians were deeply involved in the development of the human slave trade between the fifteenth and eighteenth centuries, since enslavement could be the prelude to conversion, just as the "beef Christian" Indians of the Californian *ranchos* run by the Franciscans took on board spiritual grace along with their rib eye. The *vaqueros* tending these western herds could maybe trace some of their skills in part back through Andalusian and Marisman herders to the West African Fulani of the pre-Columbian era, some of whom may have been taken as slaves to Spain. Terry Jordan, *North American Cattle-Ranching Frontiers* (Albuquerque: New Mexico University Press, 1993).

11. Alfred W. Crosby, *Ecological Imperialism: The Biological Expansion of Europe, 900-1900* (New York: Cambridge University Press, 1986).

12. Terry Jordan, op. cit. In light of Mexico's slave shepards discussed below, note Jordan's estimate.

13. Bertrand Russell, *A History of Western Philosophy* (New York: Simon and Schuster, 1945).

14. Donald Worster, *An Unsettled Country: Changing Landscapes of the American West* (Albuquerque: University of New Mexico, 1994). See particularly the chapter, "Other People, Other Lives." Seton's calculations are discussed by Worster.

15. Alexander Cockburn, "Grisly Fate of Ursus Horribilis," *The Nation* (July 1995).

16. See Worster, op. cit.

17. Edward Everett Dale, *The Range Cattle Industry: Ranching on the Great Plains from 1865 to 1925* (Norman: University of Oklahoma Press, 1960).

18. Massimo Montanari, *The Culture of Food*, trans. Carl Ipsen (Mass: Blackwell, 1994).

19. Sigfried Giedion, *Mechanization Takes Command* (New York: Oxford University Press, 1948).

20. Cited in William Cronon, *Nature's Metropolis: Chicago and the Great West* (New York: W.W. Norton, 1991). Cronon's chapter, "Annihilating Space: Meat" is a spectacular piece of work.

21. "One native son, from over in the neighborhood of Licking Hills, started the yarn about the efficiency of the Cincinnati packers. 'Speaking of sausage,' said this humorous neighbor, 'those connecting links between hog and dog almost remind me of an affecting incident that occurred some years ago at a brisk village below the mouth of Deer Creek on the Ohio called Cincinnati. An ancient maiden friend of ours was taking a stroll on the outskirts of town one pleasant summer morning, accompanied by a favorite black poodle dog—her only protector. Walking leisurely along the flowery banks of Deer Creek, her cheek fanned by "gentle zephyrs laden with sweet perfume," she at length came to the residence of a fat and furious German, which, it was hinted, had been the scene of many an inhuman butchery. At the front corner of the house she noticed a fresh pork hanging at the end of a large copper pipe which seemed to communicate with the interior of the house. Her poodle made a jump at the treasure, but no sooner had he reached the spot than he was caught under the ear by a steel hook and suddenly disappeared from the sight of his doting mistress. She, poor soul, horror-stricken by the mysterious disappearance, rushed frantically into the house in search of him. But alas! Like Distaffiana, she might have well exclaimed, "Oh wretched maide-O miserable fate. I've just arrived in time to be too late!"

'For by the time she had reached the back part of the premises, all that remained of her ill-fated poodle was a blue ribbon which she had tied around his neck, seventy-five links of fresh sausage, and a beautiful black woolly muff.'" T.D. Clark, "Kentucky Yarn and Yarn Spinners," *The Cincinnati Times-Star*, Centennial Edition, Vol. 10 (April

25, 1940) No. 100. "Business, Industry, Kentucky Section," p. 6. Cincinnati, Ohio. From *A Treasure of Mississippi River Folklore*, ed. B.A. Botkin (New York: Crown, 1955).

22. This story is told by J. Frank Dobie, in *The Longhorns* (New York: Bramhall House, 1941), a vivid evocation of this breed. The pastorals included stories of escape. A steer called Table Cloth had dodged the shipping pens for over a decade: "After returning from marketing the last fall shipment, the boss proposed that certain men take their Winchesters and bring in Table Cloth's hide and carcass. He thought he was offering an opportunity for big sport. He was surprised at the opposition that rolled up.

"Hadn't Table Cloth fairly won life and liberty? For fifteen years now the whole Shoe Sole outfit had been after him—and he was still free. He was getting old. He had never really tried to kill a man. He had simply outplayed his opponents. He could not be called mean. . . . By God, he deserved to live among the cedars and canyons he loved so well— and the boss agreed." Dobie was a wonderful writer. His description of the Texas brush country in Chapter 17 is a particularly gem of landscape literature. Worster writes, "Domesticated creatures like cattle and sheep have . . . been vital to the western experience, and we have hundreds of books and articles on the industries that raised those animals for slaughter. The animals themselves have seldom if ever appeared in that literature as anything resembling Black Elk's 'Four-legged people.' . . . The shining exception to the general cowlessness of the range histories is J. Frank Dobie's *The Longhorns*, which gives a full, appreciative account of that breed's instinct, habits and psychology—an animal, Dobie writes, that refused to be 'dumb driven cattle' but insisted on following 'the law of the wild, the stark give-me-liberty-or-give-me-death law against tyranny,' a behavior that got them labeled 'outlaws' and replaced by more docile Herefords." Worster adds, "Even Dobie has trouble maintaining any interest in cows that are not so wild or so much a maverick."

23. On antivivisection, see two entries from the *Encyclopedia Britannica* (11th edition), 1910-11. The antivivisection movement was very strong at that time, and the editors felt it necessary to print a six-page, 9,000-word defense of vivisection, by Stephen Paget, F.R.C.S., Surgeon to the Throat and Ear Department of Middlesex Hospital and honorary secretary of the Research Defence Society.

"It may be interesting," Paget writes at one point, "to compare the pain, or death, or discomfort among 86,277 animals used for experiments in Great Britain in 1909, with the pain, or death, or discomfort of an equal number of the same kinds of animals, either in a state of nature, or kept for sport, or used for the service of human profit or amusement. But it would be outside the purpose of this article to describe the cruelties which are inseparable from sport, and the killing of animals for food, and from fashion; neither is this the place to describe the millions of mutilations which are practised on domestic animals by farmers and breeders. As one of the Royal Commissioners recently said, the farmyards, at certain times of the year, simply 'seethe with vivisection.' The number of animals wounded in sport, or in traps, cannot be guessed. Against this vast amount of suffering we have to put an estimate of the condition of 86,277 animals used for medical science. Ninety-five per cent of them were used for inoculation. In many of these inoculations the result was negative: the animal did not take any disease, and thus did not suffer any pain. In many more, e.g. cancer in mice, tubercle in guinea pigs, the pain or discomfort, if any, may fairly be called trivial or inconsiderable. It could hardly be said that these small animals suffer much more than an equal number of the same kind of animals kept in little cages to amuse children. . . ."

The equally lengthy essay on furs, by Walter Parker, Deputy chairman of the fur section of the London Chamber of Commerce, had this detailing of sales at what was the headquarters of the fine fur market, the public auction sales in London. The figures are for the year ending on March 31, 1906; total number of skins in each category. Badger, 28,634; Badger, Japanese, 6,026; Bear, 18,576; Beaver, 80,514; Cat, Civet, 157,915; Cat, House, 126,703; Cat, Wild, 32,253; Chinchilla (La Plata, known also as Bastard), 43,578; Chinchilla (Peruvian finest), 5,603; Deer, Chinese, 124,355; Ermine, 40,641; Fisher, 5,949; Fitch, 77,578; Fox, Blue, 1,893; Fox, Cross, 10,276; Fox, Grey, 59,561; Fox, Japanese, 81,429; Fox, Kit, 4,023; Fox, Red, 158,961; Fox, Silver, 2,510; Fox, White, 27,463; Goats, Chinese, 261,190; Hares, 41,256; Kangaroo, 7,115; Kid, Chinese linings and skins equal to, 5,080,047; Kolinsky, 114,251; Lamb, Mongolian linings and skins equal to, 214,072; Lamb, Slink, 167,372; Lamb, Tibet, 794,130; Leopard, 3,574; Lynx, 88,822; Marmot, lining and skins equal to, 1,600,600; Marten, Baum, 4,573; Marten, Japanese, 16,461; Marten, Stone, 12,939; Mink, Canadian and American, 299,254; Mink, Japanese, 360,373; Mouflon, 23,594; Muskrat or Musquash, Brown, 5,126,339; Muskrat or Musquash, Black, 41,788; Nutria, 82,474; Opossum, American, 902,065; Opossum, Australian, 4,161,685; Otter, River, 21,235; Otter, Sea, 522; Raccoon, 310,712; Sable, Canadian and American, 97,282; Sable, Japanese, 556; Sable, Russian, 26,399; Seals, Fur, 77,000; Seals, Hair, 31,943; Skunk, 1,068,048; Squirrel, 194,596; Squirrel linings, each averaging 126 skins, 1,982,736; Tiger, 392; Wallaby, 60,956; Wolf, 56,642; Wolverine, 1,726; Wombat, 193,625.

The chief exceptions to this list were the Persian and Astrachan lambs, also ermine and Russian squirrels. These were processed and sold in Russia and Germany. All told, about 24 million creatures. The maximum from an elephant's tusk was eight ivory billiard balls, so in that same period many thousands went down each year.

24. For material about Tryon, Oswald, Cowherd etc., see Keith Thomas, op. cit. On squeamishness, see William Hazlitt, in 1826: "Animals that are to be made use of as food should either be so small as to be imperceptible or else we should not leave the form standing to reproach us with our gluttony and cruelty. I hate to see a rabbit trussed or a hare brought to the table in the form it occupied while living."

25. For material on the Nazis and their attitude to animals, vegetarianism, vivisection etc. see the excellent essay by Arnold Arluke and Boria Sax, "Understanding Nazi Animal Protection and the Holocaust," in *Anthrozoos,* 5 (1), 1992, also correspondence the following year. Arluke and Sax review a wide variety of material on these themes. *Anthrozoos* is put out by the excellent Delta Society, based in Renton, Washington. The Society encourages the matchup of old or disabled folk with appropriate dogs.

26. Elinor Melville, *A Plague of Sheep: Environmental Consequences of the Conquest of Mexico* (New York: Cambridge Unversity Press, 1994). My account of the Valle de Mezquital is drawn from this impressive piece of scholarship.

27. Alan Durning and Holly Brough's "Taking Stock: Animal Farming and the Environment," *Worldwatch Paper 103,* (July 1991). A very useful essay, with much data on raising and consumption of livestock, and good discussion of environmental consequences.

28. Terry Jordan, op. cit.

29. For an account of the exploitation of the Oglalla aquifer, see Donald Worster, op. cit., particularly the chapter, "The Warming of the West." All predictions of global warming should be treated with reserve, with caution increasing with the supposed precision of the forecasts.

30. Susanna Hecht and Alexander Cockburn, *The Fate of the Forest: Developers, Destroyers and Defenders of the Amazon* (New York: Verso, 1989). Paperback (New York: HarperCollins,1991). This contains an extended discussion of Amazonian deforestation and its causes.

31. The following examples are taken from During and Brough, op. cit.

32. Hog farming in North Carolina has been the subject of some fine journalism, notably David Cecelski and Mary Lee Kerr's "Hog Wild" in *Southern Exposure,* (Fall 1992), and an excellent five-part series published by the *Raleigh News & Observer,* first published February 19-26, 1995, reprinted March 19, 1995.

33. Tim Ingold, "From Trust to Domination," in *Animals & Human Society,* ed. Aubrey Manning and James Serpell (New York: Routledge, 1994).

34. As with organically grown produce, there are purchasing co-ops and kindred organizations that seek out free-range animals, humanely raised. This doesn't deal with the moral absolute, but it does address less environmentally destructive, smaller scale, and ultimately more equitable forms of production. Not the full bill of rights to be sure, but a slightly more elevated bill of fare.

GROWING UP ON THE SAME BLOCK AS A SLAUGHTERHOUSE

Hersham 1960-1967

The peculiar thing about living in Hersham was that St. Georges Hills, only a few miles away, was quite possibly the richest place per capita on earth. That was the contrast: living next to a slaughterhouse, or living next to a private golf club even John Lennon couldn't join because he just wasn't the "right class," although he lived on the hill along with all the wealthy ones. Some days we would get on our bikes and go and have a look at them. So our reality of the hog farm and the slaughterhouse was not a personal reality, but a class reality. Even within our tiny street class raised its ugly head. We were so class inbred, that although we were all working and lower middle class, a sub-strata had to be created. For example, we lived in a semidetached house (it only had four rooms) but that was higher on the class scale than a terraced house, which was stuck on both sides with other dwelling units. A semidetached, however, was not considered as good as "a detached." For a few summers, the children who lived in these various homes all played together, blissfully unaware of gender, race or class. That didn't last long. The state divided up those with "the better accents" from "the common ones," and childhood friends became separated, sent to different schools.

Our chance—our one chance—to rise above our class was to go to grammar school and be with the middle class. At eleven years old, we had to take an exam that would decide. My parents put all their hopes into my passing this exam. I didn't and went to a school for the ones who got to go to work in a factory, or got engaged to be married at fifteen. Lucky for me, my parents pretty much ignored me after that (their hopes shattered), and I was free to develop a malignant fantasy world, which could have turned into psychosis, or art. It was art. Also, lucky for me, my friends failed too. They became radical lesbians who joined the marines, professional car thieves, drug addicts who died, a rock star, and one shorthand typist. These choices were highly preferable to the other professions the middle classes offered women: wife of a bank clerk, airline stewardess, librarian, or nurse, with bank loans to buy furniture covered with plastic bags.

Behind our house was the hog farm—a cruel looking building with no windows, run by a cruel man. A dog on a twelve-foot chain always

ELECTROCUTION

guarded the building. From puppyhood to death, this dog was never let off the chain. All the time the chain would be clanking and dragging along the ground. The dog barked all night. We didn't identify with him at the time, as we were scared of him . . .

The smell of hogs seeped into everything—clothes and hair. This was not a well-run farm, and it was teeming with rats. Our cat was a great rat catcher and regarded my sister and me as other cats, too weak to go out and hunt for ourselves. So we would get "presents" of rats placed on our pillows, next to our faces. Our cat Blackie was so nice to us that he sometimes placed them there alive, so we could play with them. A living sacrifice—a gift of love. It was the horror of horrors to wake up and see a large form on the pillow, which would suddenly leap up, resurrected, and scurry under the bed. It was almost as bad when Blackie left just the head and tail on the pillow as proof of his devotion.

Because of all the rats, an exterminator from the council would come to the field next door to put poison down the holes. The next day we could find no rats, but all the moles had died. We would pick them up to study. They had long snouts, eyes like pinholes, and fur that was the softest softness. Their front paws were huge.

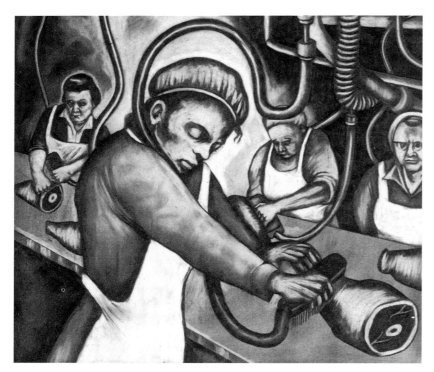

HAM SCRUBBER

A light came out of the hog farm roof and it was always on. Trucks would come at night, and there would be squeaking as the hogs were loaded. This was totally normal to us, the screaming animals from the slaughterhouse, the dog dragging the chain, the stench of the hog farm, fathers beating up mothers. My best friend's mother was beaten up so badly, she went insane. She just sat in a chair, watching TV. She never spoke, or moved. We would get money out of her purse and go to the shops and get cigarettes for her (and for us too). Violence was normal. My best friend's father died of lung cancer, at age thirty-eight, and then her mum, his wife, cheered up and was no longer insane.

Slaughtering started at 4 A.M. We all woke up with the dog barking. The pigs created the most awful racket—screaming, piercing cries, sounds like screams in an echo chamber. There would be a crashing of steel. Then toward morning, there was the heavy smell of blood, which hung in the air for two days. As a child, I thought they would slaughter all the pigs they had, then stop. I didn't understand the regularity of it.

At breakfast every morning, Dad would have his paper. On the cover would always be a lurid murder. "Sex Crazed Vicar Sacrifices Choir Boys" or "M.P. Found in Brothel Dressed in Stilettos and A Blond Wig." After he finished with it, I would get the cartoon page for "The Adventures of Rupert." For breakfast we had lard (bacon fat) sandwiches and tea. The blood had kind of gelled into jelly, and Mum had this idea that if the blood jelly got warmed up on the toast we would all get food poisoning. I told her that would happen when it got into our warm stomachs too, but she insisted that we wait until the toast got cold.

For our so-called education, we had to recite, by heart, whole chunks of the Old Testament each week in front of the whole school. If we got it wrong, we were punished. It was always Joseph begat Abraham, who begat Isaac, who slaughtered everybody. It always ended in slaughter. The point of this exercise was that we wouldn't get pregnant at age thirteen. Somehow reading the Bible and getting pregnant were the antithesis of each other.

There were four books in our house: *Aeroplanes of the First World War*, *Sex in Marriage* (with diagrams), *The Holy Bible* (with paintings of hell), and *How to Sew* (with diagrams). These books were looked through many, many times.

When my grandmother came twice a year to visit, Mum would perm her hair into little steel rollers. It was thin hair, just a few wisps. The perming stuff smelled horrifying. Then Mum would put her under a big hair dryer to cook. The result would look like an electrocuted skull.

Grandmother would look at us seriously and say, "Childhood days are the best days of your life." I resolved to commit suicide after age fifteen. If these were the best days, it was downhill from here.

We would go to the slaughterhouse sometimes, and they would give us hogs' heads. We would wrap them up, and then, as we were nasty brats, go to a rich person's house, and leave one on the doorstep. Now, later, I realize what we mistook for a rich person's house wasn't. And some poor devil got a terrible shock.

My mum would force me to go shopping with her to carry the bags. Once we went past the slaughterhouse, and a big pig darted out. We watched, mesmerized, as three men with bloodied coats gave chase. This pig was overwhelmed with dread, jumping over car bonnets in a desperate attempt to escape. We were on the main road. Between the war memorial with its huge cross and cars, there was nowhere for the pig to go. Groups of people huddled together, laughing and pointing. I asked my mum what they were laughing at, why is it funny? She said, "It's not funny. The pig is going to be slaughtered."

Maybe this was the first time I saw all was not well with the world.

THERE IS NO ESCAPE

40   S U E   C O E

GOAT OUTSIDE SLAUGHTERHOUSE

Sep 3, 1991 North Carolina, Imperial Food Products Poultry Plant
25 workers, mostly women, were killed when fire broke out. The exit doors
were locked at the boss feared chickens might be stolen. Witnesses
heard screams as people tried to force the doors open. Workers bodies
were piled up against the doorways. There were 56 injuries.
The non union wage was $11,000 a year.

FIRE DOOR

POULTRY PLANT FIRE

PIGS IN A CIRCLE

WHEEL OF FORTUNE
(AT LEFT) UP IN SMOKE

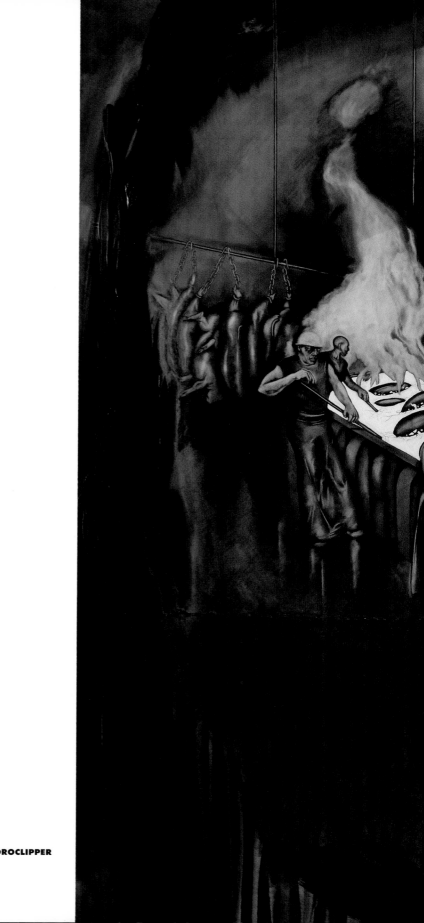

HYDROCLIPPER

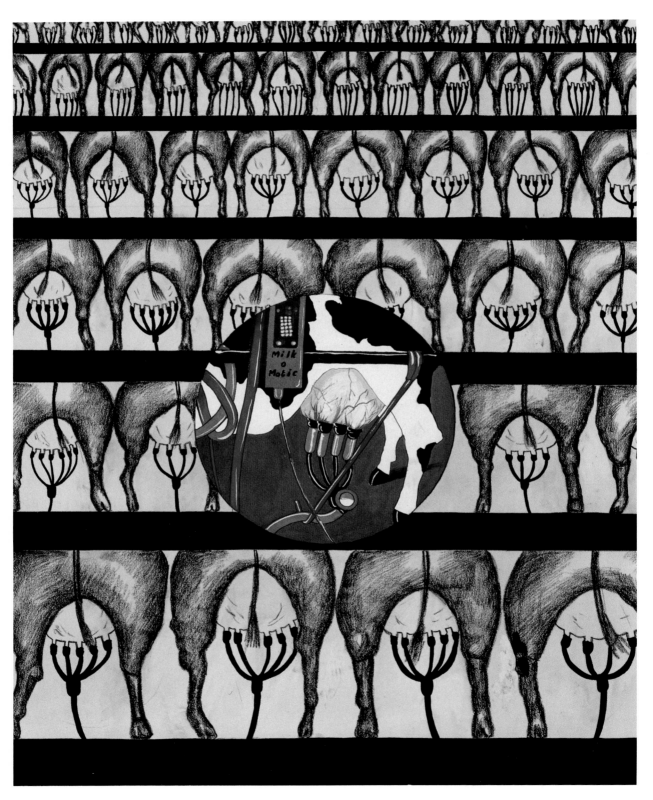

MACHINE COW

DEATH PIT

NEW YORK STATE SLAUGHTERHOUSE

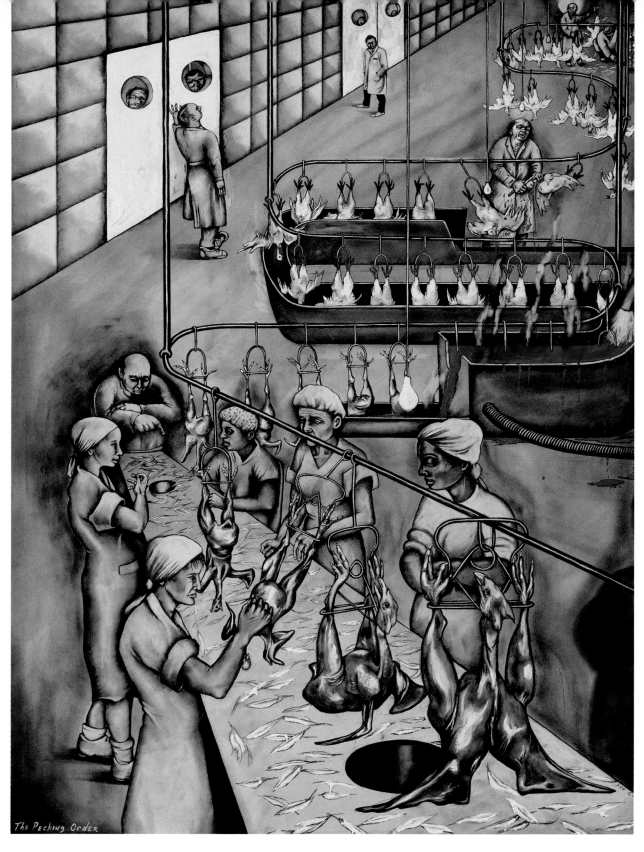

THE PECKING ORDER

Throw away Society:-
At the back of a Hatchery
in Delaware unhatched eggs
and male baby chicks are
thrown in a dumpster
and left to slowly
Suffocate or die of
exposure.

HATCHERY

COW 13

THE WAIT

LIVE BABY CHICKS AS FERTILIZER

My sister Mandy and I drove a distance from Chicago, and in the shadow of a working nuclear power station is the pig farm. It is a medium-sized, "farrow to finish" operation. In a farrow to finish operation, the baby pigs are confined in stalls until they reach their slaughter weight. The farmer and his family were pleased to get visitors. They were thrilled in fact to show us around, even though we were total strangers and had the barest thread of contact with this community. The farmer owned the land with his father, who is too old to farm. He helps out with the small jobs. The young farmer had been to agricultural college and knew everything about pharmaceuticals, but didn't know anything about pigs. He had accidently dropped his ball into the farrowing house and discovered that the pigs liked "to play." He was amazed that this play prevented tail biting and other destructive behavior. Mandy and I acted like this was news to us.

This farm, like most others in the area, has been in the family for generations. But now it is almost economically impossible to keep going. This family is lucky to break even. They've survived by diversifying. They also grow soy and wheat. If hog prices are bad, they have soy as a backup. We looked at all the hogs, piglets, farrowing crates, etc. It was very cold

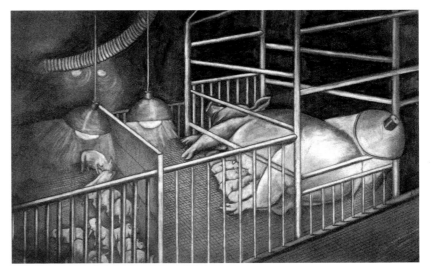

NURSERY

outside, very hot inside. The farmers dread one disease that can wipe out every pig overnight. We walked over to the farmhouse, and I stroked the numerous cats. The farmer came up and picked up a cat by the back leg, in one swoop, as he is used to picking up hogs in this way. I asked him if he picks up his kids like this, yanking them up by the back leg. (I didn't think this cat liked being swung upside down.)

We went over to the farmhouse. Tea and cakes had been prepared, with the best silver and plates. We had a great time, talking about politics. They gave me a bit of material, some hog magazines, and names of places like the Pork Expo. They were very interested in chatting about news. At one point, they got out an American flag that had hung over the congressional building in Washington D.C. We were supposed to worship the flag, but I could barely hold Mandy back, as she likes burning them. Although we are worlds apart, we got to be friends with this family, and I get Christmas cards and photos from them.

After tea, I made lots of drawings of pigs. The farmer was fascinated that the drawings actually looked like his pigs. Later that day, I gave a talk at the Museum of Contemporary Art in Chicago. A woman in the front row said, "Your paintings are so realistic, I can almost smell pigs!" (I was wearing the same clothing I'd worn at the farm.)

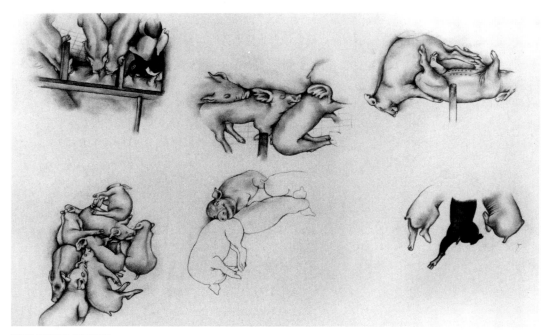

FREE RANGE PIGLETS
(AT RIGHT) FACTORY FARM

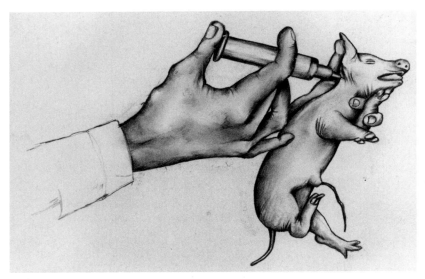

A FEW MINUTES OLD

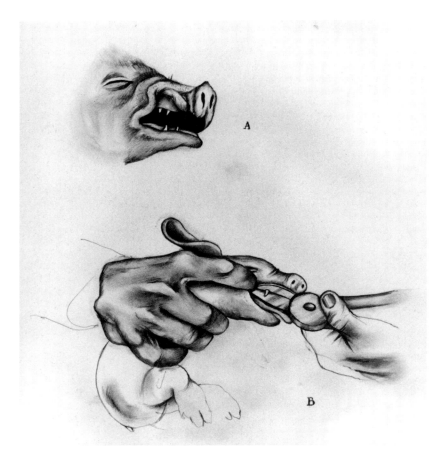

TEETH CUTTING

The feeding lots for cows look like the stocks, an old English device which secured a criminal, whilst the townspeople pelted him with garbage.

As soon as I get off the plane, I can smell the slaughterhouse and feedlot down the highway. A bit further into town, the odor is very strong. I go inside the dairy with a young man who lives in the area and speaks Spanish. The smell comes from 1,500 cows in a small field. The foreman is a very nice man and shows us around very openly. But he avoids certain questions, such as the life span of a cow in this situation, and how many cows have mastitis. It is a very odd place. The cows in the field are filthy. The dairy itself is spotless, automated, computerized. There are only four workers—all Mexican. The foreman keeps the records very proudly, in old fashioned accounting books, in a delicate script. Each cow is accounted for and has a number. Apparently, these workers don't take to computers. I look down the column of cows and see birth and morte, the short lives, every detail about each cow, how much milk each gives, and, if not enough, then the date each cow was sent off to the slaughterhouse.

The cows are herded in and put on automated milking machines—mechanical cows. There is a sucking hum. We go into an adjoining room, where there is a giant milk vat high above with a thick pipe leading up to it. The foreman tells me to put one hand on the pipe and one on the vat. And it's amazing! The pipes are as warm as the milk coming out of the cows, and the vat is so cold that it instantly chills the milk. All these cows had their calves taken from them at birth and fed an artificial milk substitute. If the calves are male, they become veals, and if female, milking cows, like their mothers. All so we can drink government subsidized milk, which is too high in fat for humans. The government buys all dairy surplus to keep prices artificially high. This subsidy costs the public between $400 million to $1 billion a year. And yet diets heavy in animal fats have been linked to a higher incidence of heart disease, strokes, and some kinds of cancer.

FEEDLOT

The boss wouldn't let me draw or take photos in the slaughterhouse, so I wrote this a day later. Veal calves are slaughtered in lots, each lot containing ten to twenty veals. The calf is three to four months old at slaughter and weighs between 250 and 300 pounds. Veals are kept off feed for eighteen hours before slaughter and handled with care to avoid bruising. Veals have to be dragged to the slaughterhouse, as they are too weak to stand and walk.

The animals are forced into the restraining pen, two at a time. The veals can see their comrades having their throats cut. The calves' eyes become practically white. Foam is pouring out of their mouths.

The man with the stun gun waits until there is enough space in the conveyor belt to receive the newly stunned veals. A large metal bolt strikes through the animal's skull. People who think this is a "humane," painless process are deluding themselves.

According to the meat industry's handbook, *The Meat We Eat*, twelfth edition, veal calves struggle for a longer period after sticking than other classes of livestock, so it is good to hoist them. The veal is hung upside down by a chain, and the throat is slit. The animal bleeds to death, which takes up to five minutes, as it moves along the conveyor belt.

The head is taken off. The body is slit open and steam comes out with all the entrails. Hooves come off. The carcass is cut into parts.

The conveyor belt starts up and all the bodies move down one. I see one calf with its throat slit, #6 on the conveyor belt, move one front leg in a last movement. This must have taken a massive effort as its body was drained of blood—a denial of death. The inspector wore a face mask.

The owner of the veals gives twelve dollars to the owner of the slaughterhouse for killing them. I keep bumping into the inspector, he pops up all over the place. The inspectors all look like surgeons, and they are clean of any blood. They are government employees.

The "jobber" is the person who chooses the best pieces of freshly slaughtered meat and transports them to the sales people. A jobber and I look into a giant vat full of brains, maybe 300 brains. Larger than human brains, they are white with blood clots. We look into another

THROAT CUTTING

vat and the jobber tells me, "that's all livers." They are very large and yellow. He says yellow liquid oozes out of them, which means they have been pumped up with hormones. There is a long line of workers as far as the eye can see. They cut meat off bones and ribs. They work so fast I can't see their hands moving. The forty full-time union workers get fifteen Canadian dollars an hour and kill 1,000 to 3,000 head a week.

COMPRESSION STUNNER

ABATTOIR—MONTREAL

This slaughterhouse is thirty-five minutes from the center of Montreal. We drive along the highway in a freezer truck, go through a housing estate, then onto a deserted road, along which are several meatpacking buildings. These buildings look typically innocuous. They are one-story link and corrugated structures, with no clue as to what goes on inside, except for the stream of trucks backing in and out. We go into the front office, and I wear a hard hat and white coat. I've heard stories about this place. The boss, according to all accounts, is a multimillionaire, who closed the plant down for three years sooner than have a union. This is the largest slaughterhouse in Montreal. In the end, the union and the boss came to an agreement. Workers in bloodstained coats come in and out of the office. They all have cellular phones. They are taking orders from jobbers. Cattle and veals are to be slaughtered in ten minutes, so advanced orders are being taken. The men have white hair nets on under their hard hats. One of the jobbers tells me to get rid of my hair and tuck it up under my hat. The boss's daughter glides by, looks at me and then says to my guide Ian, "What's *she* doing here?" Ian says that I am his new assistant, and he wants to show me the kill floor. All the white workers here are Greek, in fact Greeks control most of the meat production in Montreal. The majority of Greeks speak fluent English and are second generation. This differentiates them from French Canadians, who generally don't speak English. There are also many African Canadians.

New trucks drive up to the back, and Martin, my fellow assistant, says jokingly, "It's their last journey." Martin has a lot of physical work to do, carrying carcasses and "sweetmeats." We go into the main room, which has a vast conveyor belt. It has two levels, on the top are the cut-up pieces of meat, on the bottom, rib cages and big bones. Along one side are workers, mostly Black, wearing hair nets and white clothes. They are cutting, chopping, slicing, and throwing the neat bits on the top belt. When I watch this, I can't believe humans are capable of this type of labor. It's just so hard. The conveyor goes so fast. I know they are making about 1,500 cuts an hour. I understand why these workers get carpel

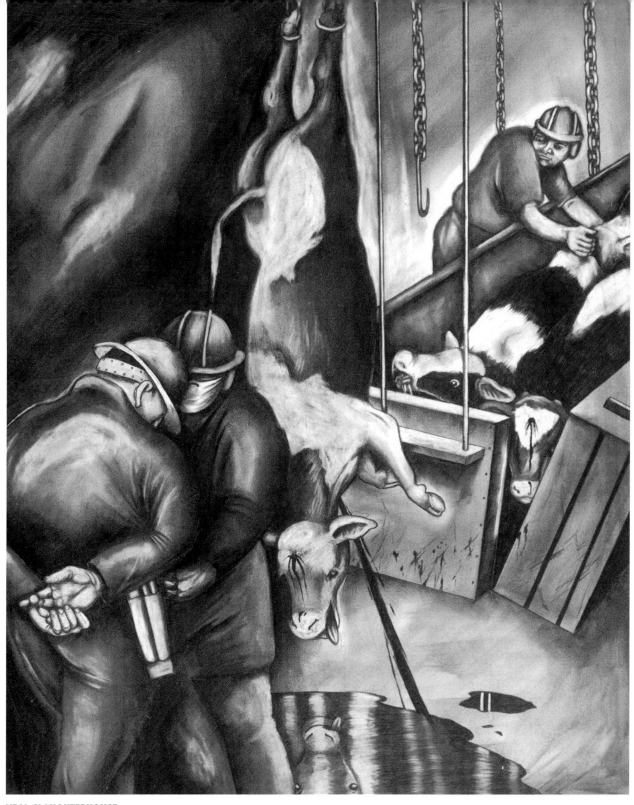

VEAL SLAUGHTERHOUSE

tunnel syndrome, because these are the same forceful movements over and over. I wonder what it's like in the winter here. This meat is cold, having come from the cooler. This reminds me of when I worked in a factory, the mind-numbing boredom, the hypnotic effect of counting the minutes until the break. It's like splitting yourself up into parts.

I see no older workers. How would it be possible to do this labor, over the age of forty? They have to stand all day in ice water and blood. When they get home, all they can do is eat, maybe watch TV, and sleep, before it starts all over again. A loud buzzer sounds and the workers disappear, everything stops. It must be the break. The meat inspectors are wearing protective eyewear, hard hats, and earphones. They patrol everywhere, looking and listening.

We go into a huge room through a very heavy door, like the door of a safe. I look down, and I'm standing on a grid drainage floor. There is a conveyor belt with the corpses of cows and a large steel table, where one worker is scooping out brains and throwing them in a steel cart. There is a lot of crashing metal and shouting, and all the men are wearing ear protection. The corpses swing along with speed, the weight giving the impetus to move. I suppose the tracks on the ceiling must be at an angle to allow for momentum. The intestines, brains, livers, and kidneys are being taken out and put in steel carts with wheels. I'm told these parts are valuable, and there are thousands of dollars worth in each cart. The organs are yellow with blood spots. Maybe there are 500 brains in one cart and 500 livers in another and so on. Many tongues also. I keep thinking of the phrase, "They cut out their tongues, to stop them talking."

The room is quite dark. I always thought my memory of past slaughterhouses was colored by my emotion, but I can see now that the hanging, moving corpses obscure the overhead lighting. I wish I could take photos, but that would compromise Martin and Ian who have to work here, and they are taking a risk as it is. The workers drag and cut out innards, standing on a raised platform. And the liquid and guts drip and fall through the grid to the floor below. There is steam, as the hot intestines come out. I think there are about five workers doing this with an inspector watching. There is nowhere for us to stand, since we don't have a specific job to do. I am walking carefully on the grating, as it is slippery. Ian opens another door, a really heavy steel one, and we are on the kill floor, also called the "hot floor" because the animals' blood is hot, and the rest of the packing plant is kept cool.

In fact, the animal goes from being alive and hot, through different cooling procedures, until it's frozen in the butcher shop or supermarket. Meat that doesn't go through these stages is called "hot meat" by the industry. Although not illegal, this meat hasn't cooled sufficiently to cut it cleanly and hasn't obtained a red, crisp appearance. The meat is dangerous to the workers, because it is hard to cut. Hot meat happens when the demand exceeds the supply, and the carcass is rushed through.

There is no place for observers to stand on the kill floor, so we have to keep moving and ducking under the swinging corpses, which move along very fast. The workers slow down to allow us to stand somewhere. I realize the meat inspector has to constantly do a balancing act along the raised platform where the workers stand.

A huge steel door opens, and two calves are forced through with an electric prod. They are pushed into a restraining crate, a metal box. It is very hard for them to squeeze in, and they don't want to, as they can see everything and it scares them. It takes a long time to force them. Veals can barely stand anyway, because they have lived their short lives in a crate and been given only milk to drink, no roughage to build bones. So their bones can't support them. The veals' fur is usually caked with diarrhea. The person on the other side of the restraining crate is getting frustrated, because the veals won't move all the way inside. They are two-thirds of the way in. The door keeps dropping down on them. It's a steel door, and it keeps rising up and dropping. It crashes down on their backs again and again. So the veals are getting electrocuted with the prod from behind and smashed from above. They finally go into the crate. They are squished together and can't move. I see their ears are stapled with their lot numbers. They look around wildly, making no sound, their heads are trembling, as if they have palsy.

White foam is dripping from their mouths. One calf looks at me with what appears to be trust. They wait. The worker with the either the bolt pistol or the electrolethalizer (I am not sure which, as I was absorbed in watching the animals) runs one hand from the head of the calf, right down to the flank. I am mesmerized by this action, so much so, that I didn't see him shoot the calves. Now we are in the second stage of the killing—the "sticking." I look down and realize I am standing on the drain for the blood. The drain is made out of wire mesh, and although I can't see it, I know the blood is going into containers under the floor. There is no heavy odor of blood, which exists when the blood is drained directly into water.

One stunned veal swings towards us, hanging upside down, chained by the legs. I have seen a lot of animals not properly stunned before throat cutting, but this one is stunned. It's a misconception that animals are dead at this stage. It's important that the heart pumps the blood out of the animal, once its throat has been cut. Every time I go to a slaughterhouse, I try to see aspects I have missed before. In this case, I pay particular attention to the sticking. The tongue hangs out of the mouth. The man cuts the carotid artery. Because of the weight, this hole becomes elongated, looking like the throat has been cut, but it has not. The blood comes out like a red glass rod, a moving, solid rod. The next stunned veal is waiting to come down the line. I am thankful not to be splattered with blood, but notice my shoes are covered, and I am standing by slivers of flesh. The veal then swings along the line, with a slight push, and the blood continues to drip. The veals wait in line to be decapitated and to have their hooves cut off by power tools. As I watch, I see one veal that is about to be decapitated—alive. Although almost completely drained of blood, this veal has come out of the stun, which means there was not enough electricity or the captive bolt did not hit the right point.

Before decapitation is "rodding the weasand" (esophagus), which means separating the esophagus from the stomach to prevent the contents of the stomach from spilling. (The contents will make a mess and taint the meat.) The abdomen comes out, separated from the trachea. The esophagus is tied off. As I'm watching the "continuous, mechanical-powered rail system," the veal moves down from rodding to decapitation. In this case, I'm watching "dressed veal," a veal that hasn't been skinned. I hope by this time the veal is dead. I can see the front legs move, like an animal dreaming, when the limbs look like they are running in slow motion. This poor, pathetic veal can have no memory of actually running, because it was restrained in a crate for its entire life. As I leave the kill floor, I touch a veal. The fur is so soft and long, silky almost. I thought it would be coarse. I touch the ears and realize the last heat is leaving the face. What was alive a few moments ago in helpless misery is now dead, an eight-inch bolt fired into its brain. A power clipper takes off the head in two snips, another clipper takes off hooves— four snips for four hooves. They clatter to the steel mesh. These are hooves that never ran or walked on grass. This creature was kept in darkness its entire life, to keep that flesh tender and white on this day. Someone calls out, "That's the end of the veals. Cattle next." A buzzer sounds and the line stops.

VEAL SKINNER

I ask Martin about politics. He says he doesn't ever think about them. He says that he gets unemployment and works off the books at a cash job. Martin also works as a DJ on weekends—his favorite bands are Led Zeppelin and Public Enemy. He wants a car and tells me he had a cellular phone like all his friends, but his first bill was $350, so he got rid of it. His brother is getting married at age twenty-eight. The whole family will go to Greece for the wedding. Martin wonders when he will get a girlfriend, then he says he doesn't care if he ever gets one. He's twenty-one-years old. Martin shares his cigs and his soda with me. He doesn't want to do this job. It's too much heavy lifting and doesn't pay enough. When we go to look at the killing floor, he jokes about it, but then he gets upset. "It's wrong." I am amazed that although he handles the dead corpses all day, he hadn't seen the actual killing.

In a back alley, Martin unloads veals, a hundred veals, hung and unskinned. They go into a white-tiled room behind the butcher shop. There is a deep white sink, and many sharp knives neatly arrayed on the draining board. An elderly man, the skinner, waits as Martin hoists the veals on to a rail of meat hooks. The veals slide down, and the skinner expertly separates the hide from the flesh. The furry hides fall to the floor like cast-off dresses. I look at the skinner's hands; there is something wrong. I look more closely and see each finger has been severed at the joint—he has only stumps and thumbs.

LAST BIT OF DAYLIGHT

This slaughterhouse is within the prison system. The meat is produced for the prison. The slaughterhouse workers are training the prisoners to be slaughterers. I spend a long time with Bill, the head slaughterer, and some of the workers. It is nonunion, and the workers have come from other meatpacking plants which have been forced to close down. One of the workers has seen me in the company of an animal rights activist and also has seen something about me in the *Village Voice*. They are, not surprisingly, hostile and suspicious of me, as some have already lost jobs and have large families to support. Also, the local animal rights group is very actively trying to close this place down. Bill swings from very hostile behavior to pleading with me to understand his circumstances. I am in a quandary. I support the views of the local animal rights activists, but not necessarily their tactics. In general, they are from a higher income level than these workers, so the activists are less understanding about the consequences of closing the plant. The workers are very hostile towards them. In a cushy office, the boss gets none of this aggravation. He gets $80,000 per annum for doing *zilch*. Very cunningly, he has used the workers as a buffer from the activists.

The workers and I have a raging debate right on the kill floor. I sit on the steel cutting table, and the workers smoke cigs. We talk about *The Jungle* and the industry, and the fact that they can't loose these jobs. I get the impression that these workers are wanderers, wandering the United States looking for meatpacking jobs. On the one hand, they desperately need a union, but on the other, they feel the union betrayed them in past struggles. I find myself thinking that if I get too much information, too many agendas, I will never make another picture. Animals are mute. But humans can communicate verbally, and as the workers carry on talking—even though I'm still sitting on the kill floor—the animals fade away. The men's reality becomes paramount. I identify with them very quickly. They feel under siege.

The day before, I went with Bill in the elevator, a steel platform which rises over the larger animals, and he asked me if I wanted to "participate in the slaughter." I declined, although it makes very little dif-

(OVERLEAF) EXSANGUINATION

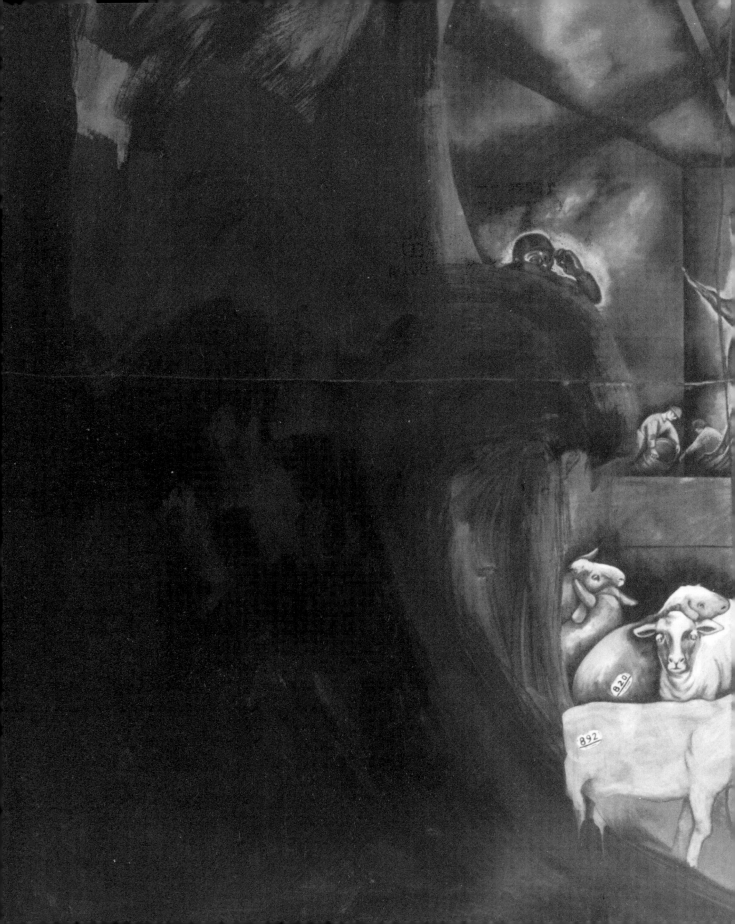

ference to the animal, since I'm standing right there. Bill pointed the bolt pistol at me and said half-jokingly, "This is to kill artists, women, and animals." I looked down the barrel of the gun and made a kind of little girl giggle, as though it was a joke to me too. I saw all the faces of the men looking up and laughing. Bill then told me that he always kisses the animals before he shoots them through the brain. Luckily at this point, the government inspector came in. I questioned him, and he knew nothing about farm animals, workers injuries, or anything. To every question I had, he replied, "it doesn't happen here." I seriously suspect he is on someone's payroll.

The next day, Bill has mellowed toward me somewhat. He now sees me as "a babe," and he gives me his cherished animal slaughtering books. *How to Slaughter Sheep*, for example. Milton Friedman would be pleased. Bill believes in the free market, social Darwinism, and that we "need meat to eat . . . it's natural." He believes he is teaching the prisoners a good trade and that the meat-cutting business is good rehabilitation. He calls the prisoners "his boys." It's a bizarre sight to enter a slaughterhouse where the head slaughterer is holding a gun, the prisoners have knives, and the guards of the prisoners have guns. I feel unarmed, along with the animals.

Bill takes me to the "chilling room." This place is the most scary for me, as I always imagine I'll get locked up with all the hanging corpses in the dark. The door is very heavy, and without a coat, it would be hypothermia for sure. The hogs hanging here have been freshly killed, despite what Bill told me earlier. I wanted to see the hogs slaughtered, but Bill said they hadn't killed any recently. He's covering up the slaughter because he doesn't want the activists to know when the killing starts— he's afraid of demonstrations.

As for politics, these men don't want to be aggravated. Their lives are so hard, the American dream so relentless that they balance in midair-with no place to land. To them, politicians are corrupt scum, and it's as though the government exists on a separate planet (which it does). Yet on a dime, they turn with the flag, joining the racism against Blacks and Jews. But they have big hearts, and I'm not generalizing about all "working people," I am talking about these four men. They are very loyal to the prisoners. Bill has adopted homeless children. But to the bosses, the lives of these workers have the same value as the lives of the animals on the killing floor.

I arrive late at night and check into a small motel. The curtains are drawn on the bay windows. I watch TV all night. At 6 A.M., I am tuned into the Home Shopping Network, mesmerized by glinting cubic zirconium on a twirling red-nailed finger. The room begins to shake, and then stops, and then starts shaking again. I go over to the window and look through the curtain. Outside the window a few feet away, a train has come to a standstill. It is a cattle train. The sun is rising. A thousand eyes are reflecting in the light, staring into the motel room. I can see the cattle between the wooden slats. They are silent and motionless. The temperature is below zero, and the cattles' breath makes a white mist.

The train starts up again, very slowly. This is the longest train I have ever seen. It takes a full thirty minutes to pass by. There are hundreds of cars, packed with thousands and thousands of cattle on their way to slaughter. Six billion animals are killed each year in the United States for human consumption. The suffering of these animals is mute. For the defenseless, the gentle, the wounded, the ones who cannot speak, life consists of indescribable suffering.

MCWORLD

A rancher named John introduces me to his father-in-law, Don, who is one of the biggest ranchers in Utah and a buyer of cattle for one of the largest animal slaughtering corporations in America.

We go to Don's ranch, a small, modest ranch situated in a massive area of land the size of Manhattan. Don is elderly, but still extremely active. He is one of the last cowboys. He has no checkbook, all his business dealings are done on his word. There is nothing gaudy about Don's lifestyle, but he is obviously a very wealthy man. Apparently, John Wayne was a friend who would visit for vacation.

Don invites me on a tour of his ranch and says he will saddle up a horse. I decline, so John and I follow him in a truck. We go up into the mountain range, which is beautiful. The cattle are in a valley. Don knows the names of every wildflower and plant and knows each steer individually. Don's two dogs look up to him with worship in their eyes. Once, when Don was riding in the mountains, his horse fell and crushed him. The dogs ran back to the ranch to get help.

Next, Don shows me his barn. He tells me that there were two owls with owlets in the barn last week, but a hunter came and shot them. We look out over the range, and Don talks about his land. It was once Indian land, and Don believes that the Indians should still own it, because they knew how to look after it. He says that when he dies, this land will be cut up into parcels with condos built on it, because his type of free-range ranching will be obsolete. In the future, it will all be intensive farming.

We watch a cow give birth. The calf slithers out, and then the mother licks it clean. We stay a distance away. If the cow is spooked, she might abandon her calf. Don says that if a cow refuses to nurture her calf, her tail is cut off to mark her for slaughtering. Don has only visited one big city—Denver—where he goes once a year to buy purebred cattle. He has peculiar ideas about people who live in cities. He claims they are mixed breeds who are doomed. John looks at his father-in-law in horror. I point out that all humans are "mixed breeds," and that all Don's so-called purebreds end up in a slaughterhouse—doomed, too. Despite

Don's ideology, his actions don't match his words. From what I've heard, he gives money, jobs, and housing to many people in need, with no strings attached. Like all the people I have met in the meat industry, he can't be categorized. His life is complex.

I WILL FEED AND CLOTHE YOU

It is hot, even late in the afternoon. I am driving in the slow lane on the thruway and to my left is a truck, an old truck, stacked up with crates maybe twenty deep. The orange paint on each crate is peeling. The crates are very shallow—I estimate only seven inches high. I speed up to keep alongside the truck . . . it is crammed with white chickens. The truck is traveling at around seventy mph, and the crates are jumping around. White feathers blow into the traffic.

These white feathers just keep blowing in the wind along the thruway. The chickens are headed for one of the many New York City chicken slaughterhouses. I get up close and see the chickens are packed

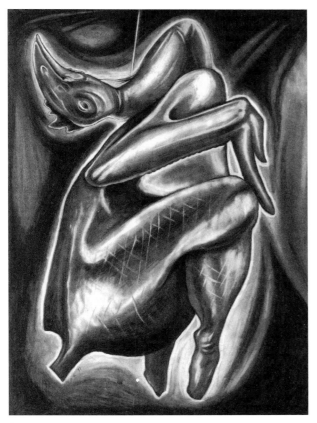

CHICKEN

in very tight. The noise of the traffic, the heat, and the speed must be unbearable to them. These birds have been kept in a darkened room their entire lives, and now they are here in the middle of the thruway. Some chickens have managed to squeeze their necks through the slats of the orange crates. Or maybe they wanted to bury themselves in the dark, under other chicken bodies, but their heads were forced out of the crates. Their eyes are looking out, unaccustomed to light. Most of these chickens are dead. Their heads, with that pinkish red crown, flop up and down with each vibration. These are the lucky chickens, the ones that die of shock before reaching the slaughterhouse. There are bizarre distortions, a limb twisted here or there, beaks agape. In this context, it's almost funny—cartoon chickens. They are buffalo wings, breaded and fried. Or plump roasted flesh with thermometers popping out to show when they're cooked.

The chickens in the crates never got to stretch their wings. Did they feel pain, did they suffer? Yes. And now their feathers are torn off in the wind to fly all over the thruway.

FORCE FEEDING

There is a very long, narrow, prefabricated building that looks like it might contain a computer software business, but instead holds a chicken hatchery. Heat bounces off the tin siding of the building. I am with Lorri Bauston from Farm Sanctuary, the activist organization focused on rescuing farm animals. Around the back is a large dumpster. Lorri and I climb up to look inside. She is looking for living baby chicks. The male baby chicks are discarded as soon as they are hatched. They have no use, no value, since they cannot lay eggs. And it would cost too much to euthanize them. So they are tossed into the dumpster alive. But it is too late for us to rescue any chicks—the sun is just too hot. On the top layer of corpses, flies are eating the chicks' eyes. Lorri keeps digging under the corpses. There are layers upon layers, some chicks still half in the shells, having broken through with their beaks. I examine a chick, so perfect with its soft yellow down and tiny wings. The chicks are thrown in with the other garbage: empty Coke cans, cigarette packs, computer print-outs, samples of our throwaway society. Gene Bauston, cofounder of Farm Sanctuary, told me that sometimes the baby chicks are ground up alive and thrown on the fields as fertilizer. Walking along a plowed field, you can sometimes find a chick, still alive, with no legs or wings.

Family of Goats — 24 hrs from slaughter — Lancaster Stockyards

FAMILY OF GOATS 24 HOURS FROM SLAUGHTER

70   S U E   C O E

LANCASTER STOCKYARD—LANCASTER, PENNSYLVANIA

I walk through the Lancaster stockyard with Lorri Bauston. She says "things have improved," since the first demonstration against cruelty to animals in stockyards a few months ago. I think that hell must have gone up a notch to purgatory, as "things" look pretty bad to me. Animals wait outside the slaughterhouse. The enclosed stockyard is very large. It might be miles in diameter. It contains hundreds of pens, which can hold thousands of animals. The animals are herded down narrow aisles and packed into pens, into living cubes of flesh. They are then auctioned off.

Unfortunately, a farm animal has no rights until she is down. So an animal can be left to suffer for a long time, as long as she is standing. Lorri and I walk down the aisles attempting to look like farmers. Since we have no official business here, we are trespassing on private property. The guys who work here are watching us. We weigh the concept of court appearances with a fine for trespassing. Lorri is quite accustomed to court appearances. Lorri casually mentions that some of the men here would kill her if they realized she was the one who organized the demonstration. I try to see what the guys are doing. This is difficult when all eyes are cast downward. I imagine they are staring at us, planning revenge. We slink along, becoming invisible.

The first animal we see is a piglet, a tiny thing, running up and down the aisle. She has been left behind, not worth slaughtering. There is no food or water for her, and we can't take her as she is "property." Lorri swoops down, picks her up, and carries her to a more visible place, in the hope she will be euthanized and not left to starve. I am very impressed with the way Lorri picks up animals. This little pig is a typical sight, although no one seems to see it. Injured animals are left to wander around stockyards until they starve to death.

The workers ignore these animals, just as consumers ignore the workers. In the stockyards and slaughterhouses, sadism is not typical, but it exists, especially where the worker is required to do repetitive work.

In the stockyard, I stand watching the goats. They are as thin as paper. The farmer who brought these goats in should be prosecuted. The adult goats form a circle around the baby goats. There are fifty in a small enclosure, and in the waves of fear, they run back and forth trampling the babies. Small family units huddle together in corners for protection. The wave is never ceasing, never ending, hooves strike out at the fallen ones. They are all starving.

I notice one female goat in particular. Her stomach has been ripped out, probably in transport. It has not come out completely, but is hanging by the fur and skin. Every movement causes her pain, I see the chewed-at nipples on the hanging skin. She keeps turning her side to the fence, offering her whole side to the rushing swirl of goats. How long has she been like this? I stay to get documentation, and Lorri goes to complain to the foreman. The goat won't be put to death swiftly, because she is still standing. I climb over the fence to keep the other goats away. A male goat is attempting to mount her in a starving frenzy. I look at her stomach. It is a deep red, inflamed hot red, and maggots are hatching in the fold.

Lorri is now on the phone to the vet. The female goat drops her head down. The stockyard boss said, "I can't touch those animals. They don't belong to me."

The Holocaust keeps coming into my mind, which annoys the hell out of me. I see this reference in so many animal rights magazines. Is this the comforting measuring rod by which all horrors are evaluated? My annoyance is exacerbated by the fact that the suffering I am witnessing now cannot exist on its own, it has to fall into the hierarchy of a "lesser animal suffering." In the made-for-TV reality of American culture, the only acceptable genocide is historical. It's comforting—it's over. Twenty million murdered humans deserve to be more than a reference point. I am annoyed that I don't have more power in communicating what I've seen apart from stuttering: "It's like the Holocaust."

Society is a gigantic Coke machine. I go up, put my two quarters in, nothing comes out. I shake the machine and then kick it. Jiggle the coin return slot. Nothing. I look around, wanting witnesses. "Look, look, I just put money in, and nothing comes out."

My quest—to be a witness to understanding collusion—has become like a mirror facing a mirror. I require witnesses. Reality has to be shared for it to be understood. Yet it is a contradiction: to witness what is concealed forces one into more isolation and solitude. And it is

Man whips downed calf
Stockyard, St. Paul, Minnesota June 91

GOE
91

STOCKYARD IN ST. PAUL

FUTURE GENETICS INC.

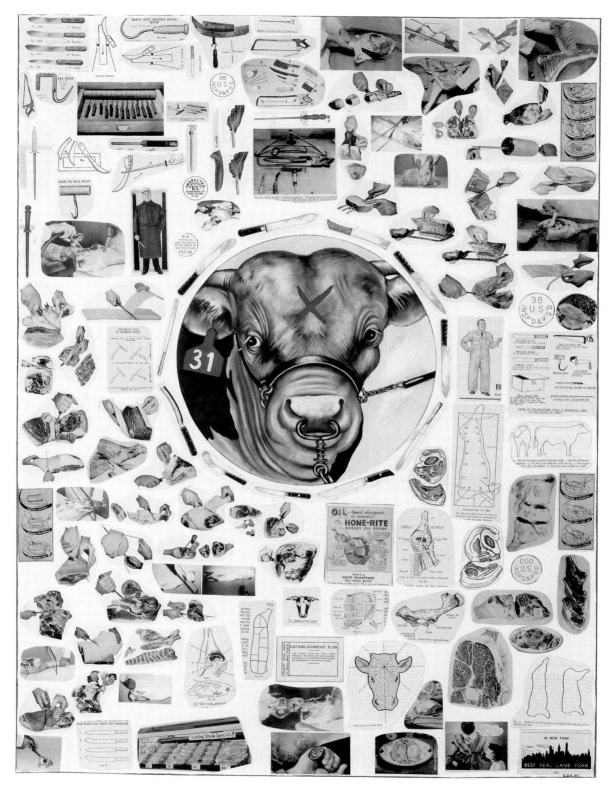

X MARKS THE SPOT

END OF THE EMPIRE

Battery Cage 18" x 20 ins.
Suffolk County Farm: L.I.
3 hens peck the eyes out of the fourth.

eggs + Food

BATTERY CAGE
(AT LEFT) BATTERY HEN

NON-BATTERY HEN

5.5 BILLION CHICKENS KILLED

UP TO SIX MINUTES TO DIE

EGG MACHINES

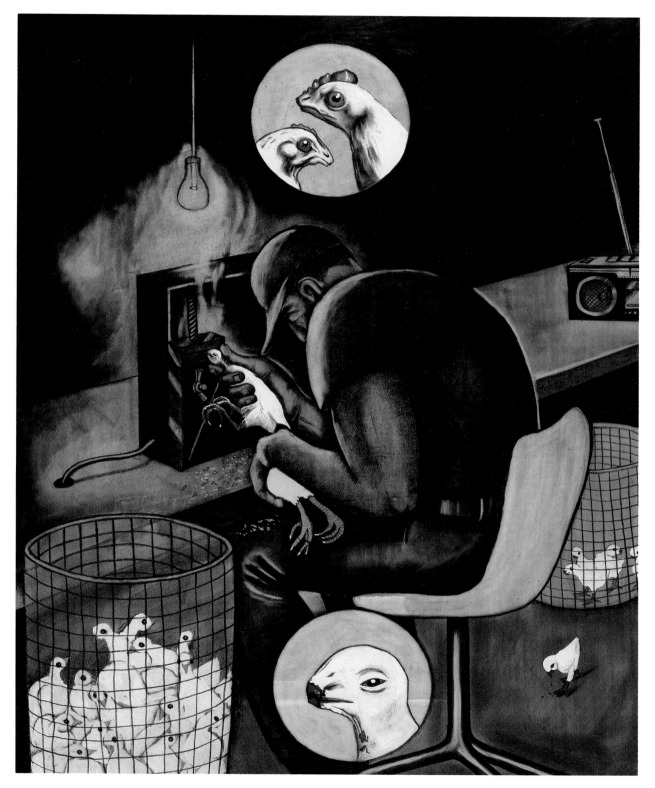

DEBEAKING

**BOYS PLAYING FOOTBALL
WITH HOG'S HEAD**

IT GOT AWAY FROM THEM
(AT RIGHT) KILLING STARTS IN 10 MINUTES

MODERN MAN FOLLOWED
BY THE GHOSTS OF HIS MEAT

ENTRANCE TO SLAUGHTERHOUSE

CO₂ CHAMBER

a *chosen* witnessing, not an involuntary witnessing. My friends are People With AIDS— P.W.A.'s: the homeless with TB, the throwaways, the human downers, the winos and junkies. They all say, "It's a holocaust, it's like the Holocaust." That is the only explanation that can be readily shared. As social beings, we desire a shared reality. The Holocaust image provides a shape, a reason, an end, a survivability.

To protect itself, the meat industry will build totally automated slaughterhouses in Mexico, for the new markets in Brazil, Argentina, Korea, and China. The New World Order will require new world resources. The old world resources have become slim plunder. Animals will be genetically engineered and cloned, so selection won't be necessary. When I started this project, I shared the little knowledge I had about gene splicing, transgenic animals, patented life-forms, and cloning, but

SUPER PIG

was met with disbelief, as though this information was from a *Star Trek* episode. Years later, this is reality, common knowledge. And it's all being marketed under the auspices of "improving human health." Why bother to limit one's diet to vegetables when Monsanto can create a low-fat cow? After all, what is a cow? A black and white docile thing? A decoration in an oil painting? An old shoe? Cat food?

When we look at a cow's face, are we looking into the face of God? A creature without an ego or a sense of self? When a calf is born, the mother nuzzles the wet calf, the calf is taken away. The mother's milk, intended for the calf, goes to us. It arrives in a carton, packed with hormones, but the side of the package proclaims: "Just Say No to Drugs." Maybe there's a picture of Nancy Reagan nuzzling a throwaway child.

Lorri and I abandon the goat. After calling various vets, none will come. I have a fantasy of offering 1,000 dollars to a vet. We go over to the pen holding cancerous pigs. These pigs have giant growths on their legs and sides. They hobble around and around on their stiff legs. One pig's eye is bleeding. When the men unload the pigs, they shock them in the eye to get them to move quickly. To the stockyard workers, it's just a job, a frustration.

What is the alternative? To be unemployed? To have the kids on welfare, or maybe homeless? None of us can handle too many contradictions. Every dollar I get drips with blood too. I look at the men again, "the guys," and see they are frightened. Lorri and I are making trouble for them. *They* will be the sacrificial goats, the bosses can always diversify. The workers are expendable, replaceable in Mexico, where they import cruelty. The concealed labor will be concealed elsewhere.

I ask the boss, "Are the workers upset by all the killing?" The boss says, "These workers see so much animal blood, they don't care, but if one man cuts his little finger, they all go crazy."

PIGS WITH LARGE GROWTHS

COLD CUTS

At the back of every stockyard is the dead pile, an enclosed area where animals that died in transit are dumped. Hunters, also, will throw any creature they have shot onto the dead pile. After the first testosterone rush, they are left with a corpse. If left on the dead pile, the animal will go where diseased animals go, into our hamburgers, via the renderers. Lorri and I walk to a large dead pile. Lorri checks to find alive ones. There are none in this case. There are skulls all around the area, and rib cages with skin falling off. The smell is very particular. It is similar to the odor of cheap perfume mingling with sweat one smells in elevators. It is a smell that takes your breath backwards down your throat. This dead pile smell clings to hair and clothes—it's the stench of death. The freshly dead animals on top are bleeding from the nose and mouth. The ones underneath have bloated up, as the gases expand in their bodies. Their legs stick out of puffy corpses.

I see a pickup truck, looming very high off the ground. On top of it is the decapitated head of a beautiful buck, with huge antlers. I guess that's why this animal had to die. The hunters are drunk and screeching. They park outside a bar and go in. I wonder where the headless body is. Abandoned in some wood? Thrown on the dead pile? I climb up on the hood to get a photo. It's getting dark. The face of the animal has frozen into a scream.

LO CHOLESTEROL BUFFALO

SPRINGFIELD STOCK MARKET—MISSOURI
(Hell on Earth).

This is an ancient stockyard. Mandy and I found it by following railroad tracks. The sun is very bright and very hot. Inside it's so dark, our eyes can't quite focus. We take turns lifting each other to look inside. Through a crack in the rotting wood, I see thousands of eyes, the eyes of cattle, looking at me. We jump down and follow our way around. There is barbed wire, ivy, broken glass, and nettles. The train tracks haven't been used in years. Around the back, we smell death and see two beautiful deer, who had been shot, slumped against the wooden side of the stockyard fence. There is a giant billboard with an advertisement for a "woman's cigarette," Capri, I think, or something like that. Next to it is a huge, flapping American flag.

We get in the building. Birds suddenly move in the rafters, making large shadows in the sunbeams that come through the holes in the roof. There are many animals inside, but it's very quiet, there are no humans. Away from the sun, it's bitterly cold, the cobwebs are frozen together, along with some newborn calves. Literally frozen together, the calves have been taken from their mothers and left to die.

We spot a young bison, the steam from his breath coming out of his nostrils like thin ghosts. He is different from the other animals because he is wild. He has a ring through his nose and makes eye contact. He makes semi-charges up to us. At the airport later, we notice cans of exotic meat for sale, including buffalo meat. But at the stockyard we couldn't figure out why an endangered species would be there. We walk around quietly, opening gates, and going along paths. There are many downed animals. We find a cow with cancer of the eye, a very common sight in stockyards. It's not in the farmers' financial interest to euthanize an animal that can still gain weight or produce milk. Cancer has eaten away her eye, half of her face, and part of her skull and brain. She is frothing at the mouth and very thin. Her one eye looks at me with what seems like sadness. She just waits. The white froth from her mouth turns into icicles.

I pick up different types of teeth from the dust, cow teeth and hog teeth. Teeth that had been beaten out or fallen out. This place must be a hundred years old. It seems full of the ghosts of millions of animals who have passed through here, now forgotten. Steam from hot bodies rises into the air, along with breath. A truck backs up and hogs are unloaded, the driver whipping and beating them to get them to move faster. All the animals tremble and retreat into their tiny enclosures.

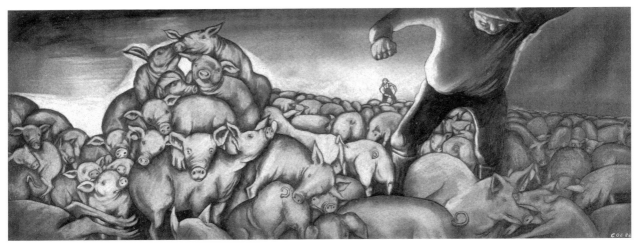

SEA OF PIGS

This egg factory is a long, bunker type building, with hen cages stacked three stories high. There are six hens in cages the size of an old-fashioned album cover. They can't stretch their wings, turn around or lie down. There is a wire shelf which catches the eggs, and a trough for food. Droppings (feces) from the hens on top fall on the hens on the second level and so on. The chickens are debeaked before they are put in the battery cage, and sometimes the tongues are burned off.

I watch through a glass window. In the cage nearest me, five hens turn on the sixth and try to peck out her eye. They have difficulty as they are debeaked and have only stumps. Nonetheless, it's relentless pecking, and the hen can't turn around or protect herself in any way. Also, their feathers are all gone. I complain to the boss, but he just says, "It's their natural pecking order." What does he care? If the hens have no eyes, they can still lay eggs.

I return on slaughter day. Two men go down the center aisle, grabbing hens by legs, wings, and necks, and stuffing them in crates. The hens are in total dread and terror. They make terrible screeching sounds. The crates are then thrown on top of each other and are left to wait in the cold for the truck. By the time the hens get to the slaughterhouse, eighty percent of their bones have been broken. The bones are very brittle, as all calcium goes to the eggs.

BRAVE NEW CHICKEN

There are no humane slaughtering regulations for chickens. They can be electrocuted in a water bath. The cheapest, most common practice is to cut their throats. It can take a chicken up to eight minutes to bleed to death. They struggle and often fall from the rail, stumbling all over the kill floor and making piteous cries.

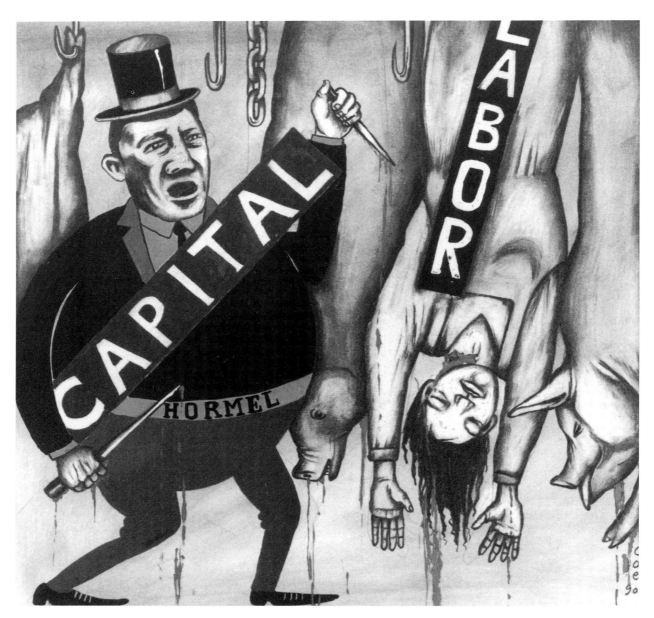

CAPITAL/LABOR

Detroit is a ghost town where the walking wounded, the homeless, and the raggedy children all hang around the only businesses that seem to be flourishing: the slaughterhouse and live porno entertainment centers. Industry has long gone, leaving behind tin housing and a gigantic tire symbolizing the dead auto industry. The architecture is Victorian. There are empty Greek-temple art museums, smashed and burned houses with remnants of decor left, bits of stained glass windows and molded window frames next to a GIRLS GIRLS GIRLS video arcade. A lot of the "girls" look like James Brown with blond wiggies.

This city has the feeling of Liverpool. A community rises out of the windswept garbage, and the people care about each other. At the center of this maelstrom is the live animal market. Crates and crates of creatures are stacked up, full of rabbits, chicks, roosters, ducks, and turkeys. I observe. People come in, look around, and make their choice. The squawking bird is brought forth from its cramped cage, its neck is broken, the creature is weighed, and a few dollars change hands.

My sister, a friend and I rescued Rex Rabbit from a live meat shop in the market district of Detroit. He cost three dollars and may be the first animal to come out alive. We put him in a box and went to the coffee shop next door. Mandy bought some lettuce, which he promptly ate. He stayed quietly in his box, looking out over the top. We put the rabbit on the counter. The boss rushes up to us and says, "Get that thing off the counter, we are serving food here!"

UNIVERSITY OF NEW MEXICO, DEPARTMENT OF ANIMAL SCIENCE

We wait until dusk and climb over several fences. In various pens, we find cows and several varieties of sheep with holes in their stomachs, and some type of permanently implanted plastic device. A lot of the devices are leaking, and green semidigested material overflows on to fur and hair. Some of the holes are big enough for your entire arm. The animals exist only to reveal their digestive systems to students. One student tells me that last Halloween, a group of students wearing masks got drunk and dared each other to shove their arms, up to the elbow if possible, into the sheep and cows. I suppose the animals live this way, crowded in small pens as living textbooks, until they get slaughtered. Their identification numbers are burned into their flesh.

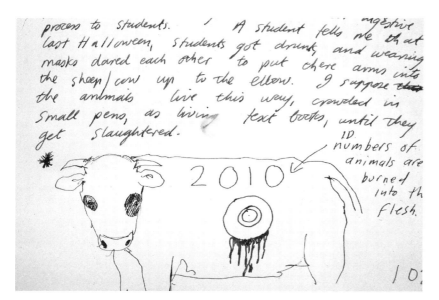

COW WITH HOLE IN STOMACH

The hogs and old milking cows wait to be auctioned off. The buyers stand on a runway over the top of the animals, choose, and then move to the auction ring. The men all wear baseball caps and overalls or jeans with checked shirts. American flags are just about everywhere. The air is full of a fine dust. I look down from the runway and see old milking cows, all used up. I have seen this many times, cows whose bones almost pierce through their hides. They have no food or water and are jammed together

THE AUCTION

like sardines. Occasionally they peer up at those of us looking at them. I see the teats are all bloodied, scarred, and they have huge lumps around the nipples, I suppose from the milking machines. A lot of small farms around here are going bankrupt, so there are many animals, most of them underweight, but few buyers. When the crips (crippled animals) go in the ring, people laugh, and bid one dollar. Most of these animals are being sold for slaughter. Sometimes they are loaded on trucks and driven states away.

FARMER JOHNS—LOS ANGELES

Farmer Johns Slaughterhouse & Meatpacking Plant is the largest in a group of furriers and meatpackers in Los Angeles. This industrial park is surrounded by highways and water drainage canals. Around the perimeter of Farmer Johns is a huge mural, covering maybe three blocks of high walls all around. It is beautifully painted, showing a happy countryside full of happy hogs. It has green trees, blue skies, fluffy clouds, fields, mountains, playing children, dogs, a farmhouse, red barns, birds, and farm animals. The hogs in the mural frolic and feed in the green grass. All the windows of the buildings are painted with similar scenes, so it's impossible to see inside the slaughterhouse. Every view is one of painted scenic beauty.

In reality, the air we are breathing is the usual afternoon hazy orange. The sky might be blue, but who can see it? There is not a single blade of grass. The heat shimmies down in a blanket of stinking meat smell. Trucks crammed with screaming hogs back into the slaughterhouse. These pigs definitely do not sound like they are dying of happiness, as the mural suggests. It's a pity Farmer Johns could not supply soothing sound effects to cover up the screaming. The workers, dressed in white overalls, go in and out. They pass through a gate where an armed guard watches us. The workers look like they've endured three shifts back-to-back. Some of them stand outside, waiting for a bus.

On our second visit, my sister and I gain entrance unnoticed. Inside the walls are large buildings for various kinds of processing, and many trucks unloading into outside pens. The hogs are prodded with electricity into the slaughterhouse. There are many crips, dying and dead hogs, that have been separated and are just waiting in the yard, some sitting in their own blood and urine. They are different from the hogs I usually see on the East Coast. They are beautiful, with huge heads and snouts and quite small bodies. I can see their ribs. The hogs are driven through in a stampede, leaving behind the ones that can't walk, or are dead. Blood drips from mouths and noses, backs are broken. They can be left in the heat for days without water, until they die or are dragged into the slaughterhouse. The industry calls them "downers."

IN A PIG'S EYE

Mandy and I have a lot of trouble getting into the place. The slaughterhouse is very old and has never been modernized or renovated. There are high walls with barbed wire and guards at the only open gate. Next door to the slaughterhouse is a graveyard. As Liverpool doesn't have any money, there is very little street cleaning or garbage collection, and gusts of cold-to-the-bone wind carry hundreds of candy wrappers, condoms, plastic bags, and beer cans like waves of garbage on a choppy sea. We can't gain access to the slaughterhouse, so we go to the cemetery behind the church. We scale the high brick wall into the back lot of the slaughterhouse. We land in a place that is, well, unbelievable. There is an enormous pile of garbage—rusted beyond recognition—under our feet. I first think it is a heap of glass, broken bottles, and stones. It is actually thousands of bones, many feet deep. Old, very old bones.

We knew that this slaughterhouse had been condemned, and we were told it was no longer in use. Then why all the security? We see hundreds of seagulls going crazy, searching over a big dumpster and occasionally diving into it. Crunching our way through the bones, we peer over the top to see layers upon layers of fresh and bloody hogs' heads. The birds are pecking out the eyes and picking off pieces of flesh. It is bitterly cold, and the heads are frozen together. We notice a man in the distance watching us, so I put my camera away, take out a notebook, and start to take notations of the architecture.

We wander over to the buildings, which I presumed were derelict. I hope to see some old slaughterhouse equipment. The windows are all broken, but steam is coming through an open door. We creep inside. What we see in there could have come straight from the nineteenth century. Two men are stripped to the waist and covered in blood. It's all over their hands, arms, legs, and hair—everywhere. There is one electric light bulb hanging over them, and they are dragging the intestines out of an animal. As far as I know, it could even be a human, as everything is coated in blood. There is an unbelievable odor of blood and shit. One man looks up and our eyes meet. He looks guilty, as though caught in a murder. It's like a scene from a Jack the Ripper movie. The building is layered with filth, walls caked with blood, floor covered with intestines and sacks.

The man asks us if the boss knows we are there. Have we got permission? I fluff through some answer. Meanwhile, I am thinking this must be the rendering plant for diseased animals, they must be dragged or led here from the main slaughterhouse. It's obviously an illegal situation. We go over to the main slaughterhouse, a huge, old building. There are hundreds of carcasses on rails and butchers buying lots of hogs, cows, and sheep.

At this point we are captured and brought into the boss's office. He asks us outright if we are those crazy animal rights people. He makes threats about trespassing etc. I say I am at the University of Liverpool doing a masters thesis on early twentieth-century architecture of abattoirs and "didn't Prof. So-and-So call first, to tell you I was coming?"

We were let off with a warning. The boss assumed we had just arrived, since we were captured at the entrance. Of course, we'd been inside for three hours.

MY SISTER AND ME OUTSIDE A SLAUGHTERHOUSE, DETROIT

THORN APPLE VALLEY SLAUGHTERHOUSE—DETROIT

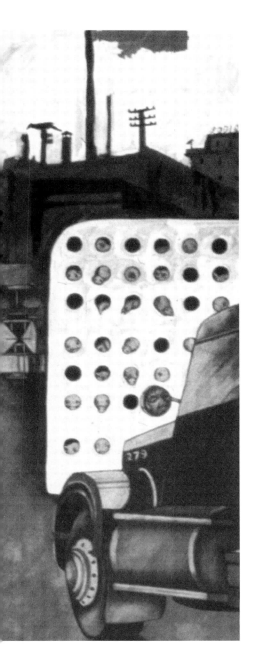

This is one of the largest hog slaughterhouses in America—1,500 hogs an hour. My sister and I waited with the hogs outside the slaughterhouse. Some hogs were having heart attacks. Some were lying on the street. They were packed in tiers in huge trucks. Hundreds in each truck. The eyes and the snouts poked out. It was freezing cold. I had no idea how far they had traveled to get there, or how long it took. There are at least twelve to fifteen trucks waiting to unload hogs. On the side of one truck was painted GO GO GIRL EXPRESS, showing dancing pigs with skirts.

A driver gets out of his truck, puts on overalls, and arms himself with an electric prod. He strikes the snouts and eyes through the slats in the truck bed. The sound of screaming is horrible. In terror, the hogs trample each other to escape the prod. They get stuck in the door, and the prod/whip keeps jolting them. I can see the hogs getting bloodied and hurt. Then the truck is empty except for some straw. They've all entered the slaughterhouse. The driver steps out of his overalls and starts to wash his boots, which got soiled when he went inside the truck to get the stragglers. The next truck drives up.

At the side of the slaughterhouse, I look up to the roof and see something so unbelievable I think I'm hallucinating. Gushing out of a large pipe—about five feet across—is a thick porridge of blood and intestines. It's pouring into yet another truck. I won't even bother to make a picture of this, as no one will believe it.

More trucks back in, another driver gets out with his electric prod. There is more terrible screaming and stampeding sound of hooves within the truck, then silence, as all the hogs have gone. The driver throws a dying hog onto the pavement and then drives away. The foreman keeps shouting at my sister and me to fuck off, so we maintain a certain distance. Later, we go into the slaughterhouse and have a long talk with the boss. I tell him that I've seen hogs being whipped as they are herded in to be slaughtered, and he says, "Damaging hogs is *very costly* for us."

(OVERLEAF) SCALDING VAT AND SCRAPING MACHINE

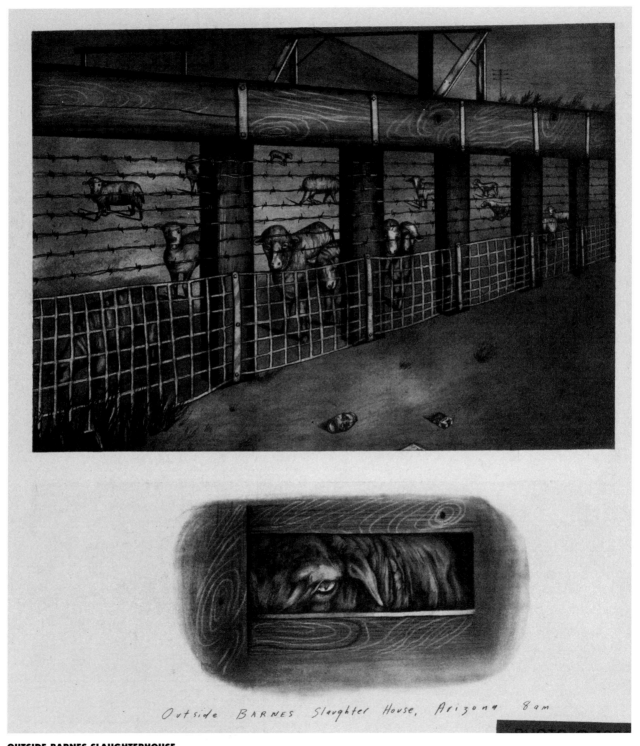

Outside BARNES Slaughter House, Arizona 8am

OUTSIDE BARNES SLAUGHTERHOUSE

94 **S U E C O E**

The plant supervisor says, "We will be killing in five minutes." At 8 A.M. it's already ninety degrees. Mountains loom behind a regular tin factory building with lots of barbed wire. There are many sheep, but no water for them. I stand by the fence, the sheep come over to me, at first one or two, then the whole flock. Such trust in humans. I reach through the wire to feel their mouths and noses, wishing I had brought water. Soon they will be slaughtered. The sheep walk away from me. My guide, Santiago, speaks Spanish and wants to see inside a slaughterhouse. He has driven me here in his beat-up yellow truck, on a long and dusty highway. There is a stray dog lying in the dust, with a smaller black and white dog. For some reason that I can't comprehend, there appears to be a piece of wood nailed into the side of a living dog.

There is a Dr. Pepper machine outside the entrance door to the slaughterhouse. I see a horse waiting. Santiago says, "They can't kill the horse, can they?" I can see no other reason why the horse is there. Locomotion in these parts is pickup trucks. I pray time stands still and we never have to go inside. We wait in the foreman's office. I look at the foreman's desk, with its paperwork and empty packs of Marlboros. Pornographic pictures of women—centerfolds—hang over the desk. They have pink and white flesh and eyes that stare out over the invoices pinned next to them. I see women walking past, dressed in meatpacking clothes. They are carrying sandwiches.

The two foremen/bosses, who are both Anglos, briskly enter the room and start to question me. I feel my eyes taking on the blank stare of the babes nailed to the wall. The bosses ask why I want to tour the slaughterhouse. I give examples from the history of art when the subjects for paintings were slaughtered animals, i.e. Rembrandt. We all put on baseball caps and go in. The foreman leads the way. The workers look up, surprised to see me, and quickly look away. They are all Mexican men. We walk through a maze of barrels and chains and end up on the other side of the rail overlooking the kill floor. The boss warns, "Don't move from this spot, it's dangerous." The ceiling is a complex system of rails, pulleys, chains, and huge hooks. The floor is wet, its grey cement sloping down to a round drain where the hoses wash the blood. The smell of blood is like a sticky face mask. It's a thick, metallic smell. In the corner of the room, I see a skull.

Two men stand fenced in on the kill floor. The older man with grey hair has a stun gun, and the young man has knives chained to his waist. The back of the wall opens up like an automated garage door. I see the feet of a man with an electric cattle prod. He is whipping two goats forward. The sunlight from the outside is blinding, making the inside seem totally black. The goats peer in. Their legs are shaking, they can't retreat. The man keeps kicking them and shocking them until they pass over the slope, and tumble forward onto the kill floor.

The door slowly closes. The older man grabs the front and back legs of a goat, swinging the goat to the ground. He pins the goat down by putting his boot on the other leg. The second goat watches and backs away as close to the closed door as possible. The younger man electrocutes the goat and then cuts its throat. The second goat cries like a child, she shakes. They drag the first goat, still kicking and writhing, into a concrete pit. It's like a sand pit with no sand. The goat slides into the pit headfirst, gushing blood. The animal goes thin like a pencil—just fur and a skeleton. His legs are still moving, and they continue for some time. The men grab the second goat and repeat the procedure. The floor is covered with blood, and I can see my reflection in it. All kinds of saws, knives, and different pulleys hang on the walls.

A white sheep with a blue brand on her side and black feet is let in. The door closes. She runs around the kill floor. The workers are by the skinning table whispering to each other. The foreman comes over to tell me they don't want any of their faces in my pictures. The sheep waits, her hooves and legs are covered with the blood of other animals. The door opens again, and two more sheep are pushed in. The outside worker doesn't realize the killing has temporarily stopped. The sheep start to bleat, soft, terrible, piteous cries. Steaming water from the hoses runs the old blood down the drain. And the killing starts again. I'm glad Santiago is here, although I barely know him and feel responsible for putting him in this situation.

Sheep bleat even after their throats are cut. They writhe. Every part of my being says to stop it, save them, which is impossible. I think of "art" and how I am going to draw it all. Will anything change when people see? This "art" thought comes so quickly after the failed rescue thought, as an attempt to comfort myself, like the idea of the "spirit"

SLAUGHTERHOUSE TUCSON
(OVERLEAF) SLAUGHTERHOUSE TUCSON—GOATS BEFORE PIGS

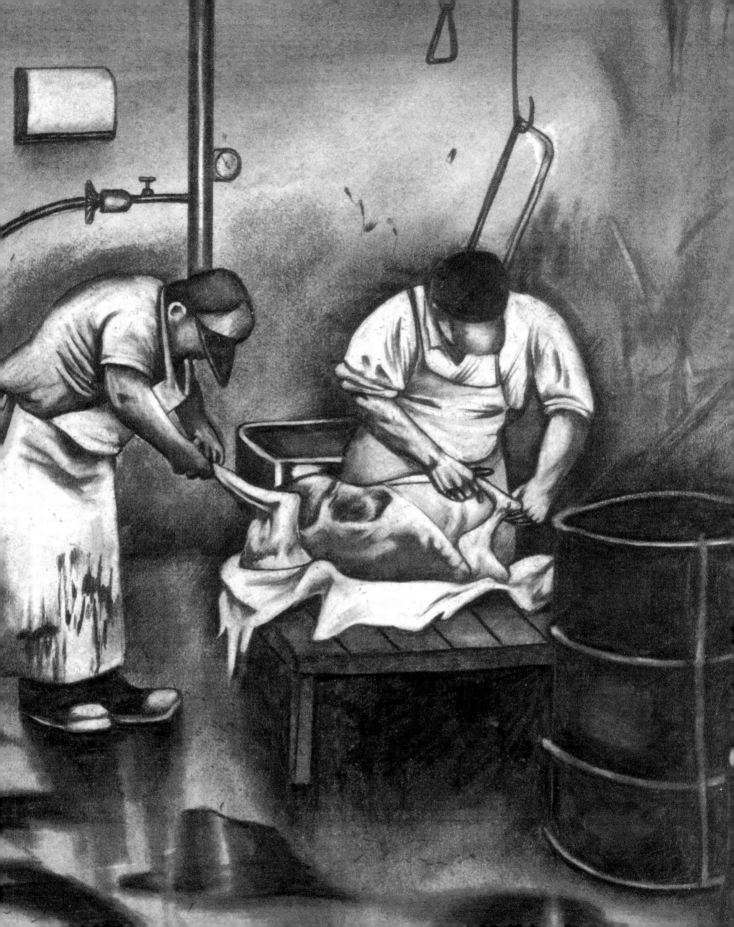

of the animal going on to another place. I feel sick and my legs are shaking—my hands too—I concentrate on acting "normal." Various animals are killed. I look for a way out.

This process is concealed. Animal flesh is a commodity, along with soda pop, toilet bowl cleaner, and Wonderbread. But watch the animal bleeding into the drain. Watch it go still. Workers drag the corpse up and heave it onto a table. Listen to the sharpening of knives. The knives have to be very sharp. The workers clip its head off and toss it into what looks like a large black oil barrel. Then they cut the hooves off and throw them into another barrel. Then the guts get pulled out, and the skin is ripped off. Skin and fur lie on the floor in a bloodied wet heap. This process takes minutes. One moment, the animal is alive, looking trusting and helpless. The next moment, that animal is in pieces in old oil barrels.

We leave the building as the cows start to go inside. The sun is blazing and the mountains look like a theater backdrop. The sheep run over to us again, but there are fewer of them. Santiago says that the men on the kill floor were more quiet and more subdued because of our presence. So we go around the back, where the corral leading up to the kill floor is covered with feces and urine. We listen through the wall. The men are shouting, Santiago says, and swearing also. This is their normal behavior. They are screaming "MATALA!" which is Spanish for "kill it!" and the female equivalent, "kill her!" As we walk away, we see a road-runner galloping along the fence. And then it flies off. This sight makes me happy, this one creature escaping humanity—for now.

Santiago says that in his home country, people raise their own pigs. The pigs live in the house with the people, get good food, are looked after, and then "when that pig's time has come," the pig is eaten. But this is America.

Several hundred cows are kept in a tiny area. It consists of a shack and then a concrete space, which is a couple of feet deep in mud, urine, and excrement. There is nowhere for the cattle to walk. I am forced to cover my mouth and nose because of the stench. Many of the cattle have foot and eye infections. Ironically, empty fields and hills surround the feed-lot. I suppose cattle use up energy, and therefore weight, grazing and walking. At the front of the concrete space is a concrete trough, full of grain mixed with concrete. The farmer comes up to me and says, "This is hamburger on the hoof."

The downer is too heavy to get up. She cries as a chain is attached to her leg, and a winch drags her along the ground to a truck. I can see her skin rubbing off, and her bones grinding into the pavement. I can see the white of exposed bone and blood. She can't lift her head up, so her head, ear, and eye start to tear on the stone. I watch the man oper-ating the winch, and he looks impatient. I start to think of school songs, so my eyes still see but my brain is occupied. At school, we sang those grinding religious ditties: "There is a green hill far away."

As she reaches the truck, the cow rolls over, exposing her udders, which are full of milk. This is the total degradation of a life.

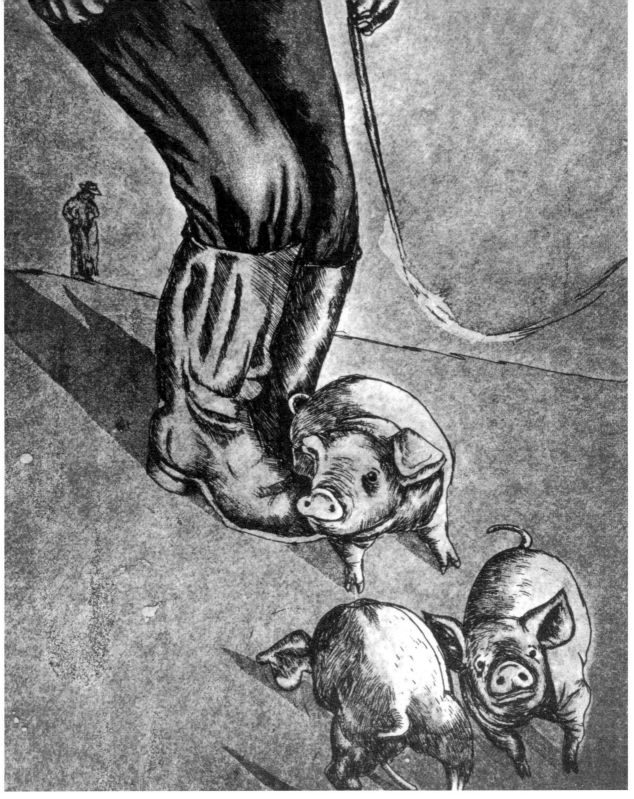

THE BOOT

There is a structure above the entrance gate which says: ARMOUR 1906. It is only original part left of the old stockyard. The place is gigantic, covering maybe a ten-block radius. Railway tracks lead to the slaughterhouse. At about 1 P.M. the smell of decaying flesh is overpowering. It's a rancid, chemical smell. They must slaughter the animals throughout the morning. The older section of the stockyard is rotted away. Roofs are off and only the skeletal, heavy wooden beams still stand.

The stockyard is filling up now with horses. They have their own section, as do sheep, goats, cattle, and hogs. The workers get very frustrated with downers. Even though it's literally "flogging a dead horse," the worker will continue to whip and kick an animal as if the sheer labor of beating will miraculously transform a near corpse into a dollar on the hoof. The animals moan in terror, but still cannot rise up. You would think there would be rage on their faces, but they are blank.

WALL STREET

Wall Street was originally an abattoir. Blood drained from the street into the East River. The stockyard became the stock market.

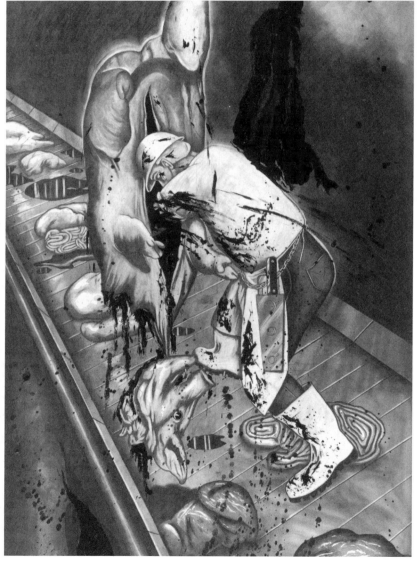

CUT AND RUN

BUTCHER TO THE WORLD

WALL STREET

GOVERNMENT INSPECTOR

UNLOADING AT 4 A.M.

SELECTION FOR SLAUGHTER

TRUCK ACCIDENT

HATFIELD P.A July 91   MEAT FLIES

MEAT FLIES

OLD COWS NEXT

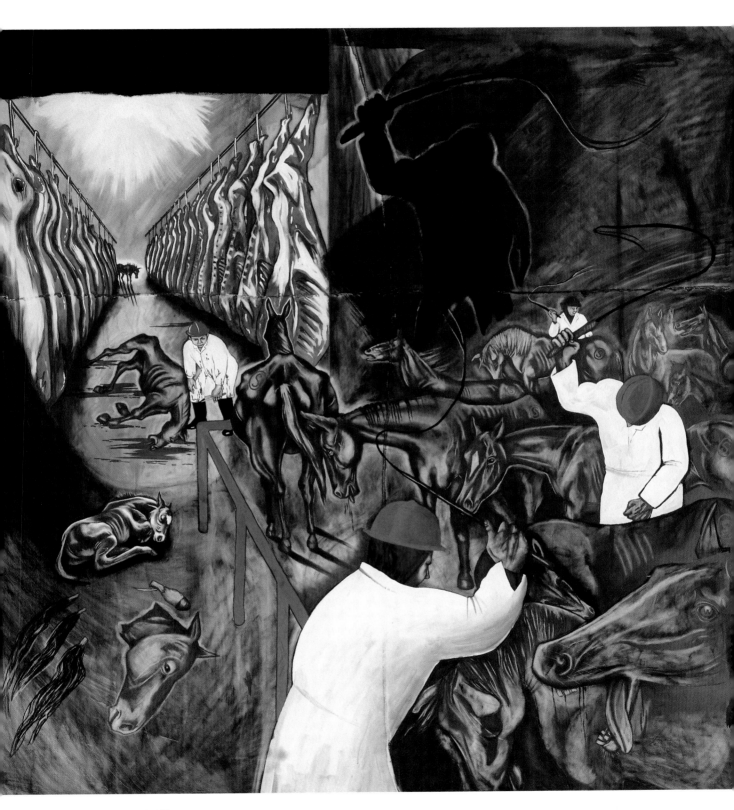

HORSE SLAUGHTERHOUSE

A downed cow, too sick to stand waits slaughter. She can wait hours or days to be killed.

SC 95

DOWNED COW

GRUSS AUS NÜRNBERG SAUSAGE MACHINE

THE BOSS CALLS IN THE IMMIGRATION POLICE

UNION STOCK YARDS, CHICAGO

"ROUND GOES THE WHEEL"

CUTTING THE COW'S THROAT

TRENTON MEATPACKING COMPANY—
NEW JERSEY

My friend Andy and I get up at 4 A.M to leave the city at 5 A.M. and at 5:35 are on the New Jersey Turnpike. It looks to be a pleasant day, weather-wise. We get there without getting lost. Although when we get to the residential street, we think we have the wrong location. This slaughterhouse is concealed with an office in front of a building and a small driveway. We find out later from the boss that the neighbors are not too pleased, as they are in such close proximity to the noise and smell, and they remember "the hog days." He and his partner, Skip, have taken over the business, and it is now kosher and Muslim slaughter only. No hogs. In fact, the word *hogs* is mentioned in a hushed breath. The boss says they do "real kosher and Muslim ritual slaughter"—not fake "like some places." Despite the smallness of this old slaughterhouse—built in the 1940s or 1950s, I'm guessing, with an old concrete floor, and a noncontinuous rail system—they handle a very large number of animals. Five hundred sheep and goats today. Because of the rail system and few workers, the slaughter has to stop after fifty animals to wait until the carcasses are dressed.

It's obviously a nonunion place, since there is little or no safety equipment, i.e. no gloves, no nonslip boots, no proper ventilation. It is medium-clean. The blood is washed into the street, maybe into the water supply. Also it smells before slaughtering. I've seen worse. The workers are multiracial, Black, white, and brown, and there is generally a good feeling of interaction. There are no women workers. No sexist insults or threats to me. The two bosses are open and friendly. The government inspector is friendly to us, but he uses bad language to the workers and speaks to some of them in a harsh way. He comes on like the boss of bosses. He kids around with a couple of the white workers, but doesn't speak to the others respectfully. I'm glad I don't work here. He has a strong southern accent, and his face looks like it has been skinned. It's white and large with exploding veins running over it, with two tiny blue eyes. He suspects that we are there to spy on him and behaves like all the government inspectors I've met so far, as a person with something to hide.

We wait in the kitchen for the truck to arrive. The workers hang out, sharpening their knives, drinking coffee, sitting in the backyard. It's 9 A.M. and the truck was supposed to be there at 7 A.M. The boss is very edgy. He says he is paying these men for doing nothing. If the truck doesn't come soon, he will dismiss them. Our hearts sink, imagining driving all the way back to New York, and then coming again tomorrow. A friendly worker, Lee, sits next to us, sharpening his knife. I draw him, and Andy asks him about himself. He is sixty-nine and is planning on moving to South Carolina when he's seventy to preach. Both he and his wife are Jehovah's Witnesses. He is a very handsome man, looking half-Indian and half-African. He tells us the world is coming to an end, and that "man is fit to rule no more." He tells us of Jehovah and everlasting life. He puts oil on a pumice stone and sharpens his knife back and forth. He has been slaughtering since he was fifteen. His son works next to him on the rail system. It's as though he's out preaching, not here slaughtering.

We asked where the truck of sheep and goats is coming from—Louisiana. Almost halfway across the U.S.A.—a three-day trip. It seems a long way to go to get slaughtered. After the goats leave the intensive farm, they go into a fattening farm for a week, prior to the slaughter. At 9 A.M. the goats and sheep arrive. The boss is relieved. He tells us the story of a similar truck from Louisiana that flipped over on the highway, killing half of the goats and sheep. Two hundred fifty killed. The boss pauses for moment, distraught, and then says, "All that money . . . lost." I imagine the truck packed with twisted bodies, and the terror of those animals. But the boss simply doesn't see these creatures as life-forms, they are the units that pay off a mortgage, they are commodities in a factory. The boss smiles and says, "But they still keep coming, thousands and thousands of them. How can there be so many?"

We go around to the back and watch the animals being unloaded. They definitely don't want to get off the truck. Whatever the hell of transportation, hell is preferable to the slaughterhouse. They huddle together. Two men jump inside and force them into the restraining pens. The area has just been power-hosed, prior to their arrival, and puddles of water have mixed with dried blood. The animals are so desperately thirsty that they try to get at the puddles through the barrier. I look at them up close. The mucus has dried solid in their noses and mouths. It's getting hot, maybe eighty-five degrees. They pile on top of one another to get away from the slaughterhouse entrance. The

office of slaughterhouse - Trenton

OFFICE OF THE SLAUGHTERHOUSE

smallest get pushed to the bottom, and the large goats scramble over the sea of bodies.

The government inspector separates them by moving gates into three sections. The animals are packed tightly. We find out that twelve goats and sheep have not survived transit. They are dragged through in garbage pails. The boss gets seven dollars for every goat and sheep he slaughters. Each one of these creatures is actually worth fifty dollars. I think of how much cash I have in my wallet, maybe a hundred dollars, enough for two lives. The meat from these animals goes entirely to New York restaurants. "They can't get enough," says the boss. The insatiable hunger of New Yorkers.

WORKING PROOF **1**   SEP 12 1991

SHEEP TRYING TO ESCAPE

The last hooves stumble off the ramp, and the truck leaves to pick up the next load. I have found a good vantage point. From the goats' perspective, I watch the slaughter. A man reaches and grabs one by a horn and drags him in. The others face the corner of the wall, all their faces going one way. As they thin out, I see one sheep. She is on her knees and can't get up. She has been crushed by the bodies of the others on top of her. I can't really draw this to do the image justice. Each animal is lifted very fast by two men, another chains the animals' hind leg. And then the slaughterer holds the muzzle closed and cuts the throat. The animals cry out, like babies. A sound between a human baby crying and a seagull. The animal struggles upside down, and blood splashes out. Five animals are bleeding and crying at once, then they are moved down the line to have their faces skinned off. Only a few feet away, a few moments away, are the alive ones—each one perfect and unique. A different face, different eyes, different in every way each from each. And then down a bit, a dismembered bloody rag of fur, eyes popping out of a splotched skull. All the same—dead parts. Lamb in the meat counter or the empty vessel that gave goat cheese.

When the first lot of killing stops, we go inside the main processing area. All the bleeding corpses are piling up on the rail. I draw a man breaking the hooves off animals with his hands. Each one goes crack. There is an elevated platform, where four men stand skinning and "fisting out" (taking out the innards). I make a lot of sketches and take photos. It's getting a lot hotter, because of the steam from all the open bodies, and the high pressure water they use to hose down the floor. The guys say you ought to be in here when it's *really* hot. The workers kid around that I'm drawing for the FBI. I watch them sneak puffs from cigarettes.

Andy and I go back outside to watch the next fifty animals. We stroke their faces, feeling like Judases. They are without any power as the gates push them closer and closer to the slaughterhouse.

PARCHED SHEEP

'JUDAS' SHEEP

▌ meet Martha Reed and her brother. She is a slight woman with very
short hair and her brother looks similar. They inherited the meatpacking business from their father, who passed away a few years ago. Both
Reeds are very nice. The whole Reed family lives on this land, which is
just off the highway. It is littered with rusting trucks and a couple of
farmhouses. The buildings are unprepossessing, low-level corrugated
structures. From our telephone conversation, Martha had me believe this
was a "small plant." I assumed that meant small animals were being killed
by a few employees. I go into the office, which is dirty and chaotic, with
splashes of blood on the walls. Just outside the office in the hallway are
stacks of barrels with hooves, livers, heads, and other body parts.

It is ten minutes before lunch break, so Martha says that would be
a good time "to get my bearings." I show Martha transparencies of my
work, and she seems to appreciate what I do, but says, "I see you are
used to small animals." We step into a large room, and I look up and
see corpses of huge, skinned animals. The fluorescent light gleams off
the white fat. I feel like I am in a bizarre cathedral. Martha fearlessly
ducks between the giant swinging corpses of beef, the falling stomachs,
and the power tools. I follow her, but tread more warily, as the floor is
extremely slick. Martha warns me not to slip. I definitely do not want
to fall in all the blood and intestines. The workers are wearing nonslip
boots, yellow aprons, and hard hats. It is a scene of controlled, mechanized chaos.

When you see how large a hanging steer is—from hoof to hoof
maybe twelve feet—and how heavy, you realize how small humans are.
The corpses are hanging high up, so the workers are on the platforms.
Like most slaughterhouses, this place is dirty—filthy in fact—flies swarm
everywhere. The walls, floors, everything, everywhere are covered with
blood. The chains are caked with dried blood. The equipment, however,
appears to be up-to-date, not fully mechanized but pretty close, and the
workers do have good safety equipment. This is unusual, so I guess this
to be a union shop. We walk on to the kill floor, and I stand very close
to the knocking pen. Martha's brother offers me a chair. But I think *hell*

no, I want to be mobile, so I stand in the doorway between where the cows are lined up to be slaughtered and the kill floor. I stand with my sketchbook. A worker comes up to me and says, "Cover your ears." I do, a very loud horn goes off, and the workers evaporate, disappear to lunch.

So I am left alone with six dripping, decapitated corpses. Blood is splashed up walls and is already on my sketchbook. I am getting used to being covered with flies, just like the corpses. But I don't like them going in my eyes. I see a movement on my right. The knocking pen is not empty, in the space at the bottom I can see the breathing of an animal. I move cautiously to peer over the top of the steel box. This is difficult, like walking on a skating rink. Inside is a cow. She has not been stunned and has slipped and fallen in the blood. The men have gone to lunch and left her. Time passes. Occasionally she struggles, banging the sides of the steel enclosure with her hooves. As this is a metal box, it becomes a loud hammering, then silence, then hammering. Once she raises her head enough to look outside the box, but seeing the hanging corpses, she falls back again. The sounds are blood dripping and FM radio playing over a loudspeaker. It's the Doors, a complete album side. I start to draw and occasionally glance back at the box to see her still breathing. When I look again, I see the weight of her body has forced the milk from her udders, and it starts to flow in a small stream, mingling with the blood. The floor slopes slightly to a drainage area. Blood and milk go down the drain. I look up and see none of the cows had been milked, their udders are still full. I know they were bought at a stockyard ninety miles away . . . but how long had they been there? Waiting, unmilked. The milk flows now, in a rapid stream. I see one of her legs come out the bottom of the steel enclosure. I could weep for this animal, but remove that empathy from my mind, just like the workers do.

Time drags on, we go through what seems like the complete hits of the Doors. The buzzer finally sounds. Then men come back and tie on their yellow aprons. There are only two men working on the kill floor. Danny does the throat-cutting, decapitating, washing the head, and taking off the front hooves, then herds a new cow in. Another man, who stands twenty feet off the ground on a platform, does the skinning with a power saw. After that the cow goes along the conveyor belt to another area.

Then I see what I rarely see in a slaughterhouse, an act of deliberate cruelty. A man, whom I hadn't seen before, comes in and starts kicking the cow's leg with his boot. He does this three or four times really hard. It's obvious she's not going to get up. I feel like screaming, "Stop that you fuck!" and probably would have, but he disappears. Upon reflection, I realize he wanted the cow to stand because she's difficult to stun in that position. Danny would have to bend into the box to get a good aim at her head. So the man had a reason for doing it. Danny gets the compression stunner, which shoots a five-inch bolt into the animal's brain. He leans over and there is a loud crack, exactly like a small handgun. I fancy I see a puff of smoke. He then goes over to a remote control device, presses it, and the side of the pen rises up, revealing the slumped animal. He goes over, chains one of the legs, and she swings up. Her legs are struggling and kicking. She swings upside down, her view of the world reversed. I had noticed that some animals were totally stunned and some not stunned at all. They struggle like crazy while Danny is cutting their throats. Danny talks to the unstunned ones as he slits their throats, "Come on girl, take it easy." The blood comes gushing out as though all living beings are soft containers, waiting to be pierced. Danny then goes next door and electrically prods the next cow forward. There is a lot of resistance and kicking because the cows are terrified to move into the knocking pen. They are forced. Danny says in a singsong voice, "Come on girl."

Once the cow's throat has been cut—it's just dripping blood now—Danny takes a knife, cuts off the front hooves in one slice, and throws them into a rubber garbage receptacle. Sometimes he misses. (There is one at my feet as I draw.) Then he skins the head, decapitates the skinned head, goes over to a sink, hangs the head on a hook, and rinses it with a hose. The head looks bizarre. The eyelids have been cut off, so the eyes stare out. Those same eyes that looked around in fear, that looked for escape, have become comically obscene like the eyes fastened to springs on false glasses. The headless corpse looks equally bizarre, the skin from the face hanging around the neck like some old scarf. Danny then pushes the line down to make room for the next. The next cow watches everything. Then her turn comes.

I watch eight cows being slaughtered, maybe more as I'm there for an hour and a half. As I watch the skinner reveal the white flesh, I see old injuries, bruises, and where the tissue has been pierced. This must have happened at Lancaster Stockyard, a notorious place. I've seen it. They have very rough handling there.

I say to Martha, "These cows seem very young to be going to slaughter. They don't appear to be milked out at all." She explains that as the price of milk has gone down, the farmers can't afford to keep them. We walk out of this place away from the flies and blood. Next door are Martha's kittens; she picks them up and plays with them. She lives in "a white picket fence house," within the slaughterhouse yard. Little trimmed bushes and trees conceal the old slaughterhouse equipment and rusted old trucks. Martha turns to me and says, "I was born here, it's all I've ever known."

BELTEX CORPORATION AND DALLAS CROWN PACKING—TEXAS

Fifteen hundred horses are slaughtered a day at this plant, for the EEC market. The market for horseflesh for human consumption is mostly in France, where it is cheaper than beef. In the United States, horse meat is made into pet food. Horse slaughtering has to be separated from the slaughtering of so-called food animals. This plant uses quarterbacks, working horses from out of state.

The first slaughterhouse is in a country area on a hill. It has received numerous complaints from neighbors for dumping blood and animal parts into the water supply. I go with an animal rights activist who specializes in slaughterhouses. We arrive too late. The yards are empty and the horses are all gone—killed—and by now in pieces. The walkway, however, is soaked in blood, showing that the injured horses had their throats cut on the concrete outside.

The second equine slaughterhouse is an hour from Dallas-Ft. Worth. It's an old cattle slaughterhouse turned into one for horses. It's wooden, with many ramps and corrals. It's on an industrial estate. Next door is a tannery, and we see the piles of hides. Around fifty horses still await slaughter. They are in terrible shape, with crippled legs and hair matted with blood. The hooves are so overgrown and swollen, these horses can't put their feet down. A horse, with a broken jaw hanging down, obviously can't eat. There is a lot of whipping. The sound is crack-crack, and as the whip hits, there is a smell of burning. We heard the sound of horses being whipped a long way from the slaughterhouse. It sounds like gunshots. The horses try to stampede away from the kill floor, and two men beat them in the face until they turn back. The boss, who is Anglo, is wearing a ten-gallon hat. The workers are Mexican and wear hooded red sweatshirts, helmets, white coats, and black rubber boots. The last fifty horses go inside.

I watch the horse with a broken jaw clip-clop almost eagerly toward the slaughterhouse entrance, head held high, lower jaw and tongue dangling down. He mingles with the other horses and disappears through the door.

My companion sees a white mare giving birth to a foal in front of the restraining pen. Two workers use a six-foot whip on the horse as she gives birth, to get her to speed up and go onto the kill floor. The foal is thrown into spare parts bucket. The boss in his cowboy hat observes from the overhead walkway.

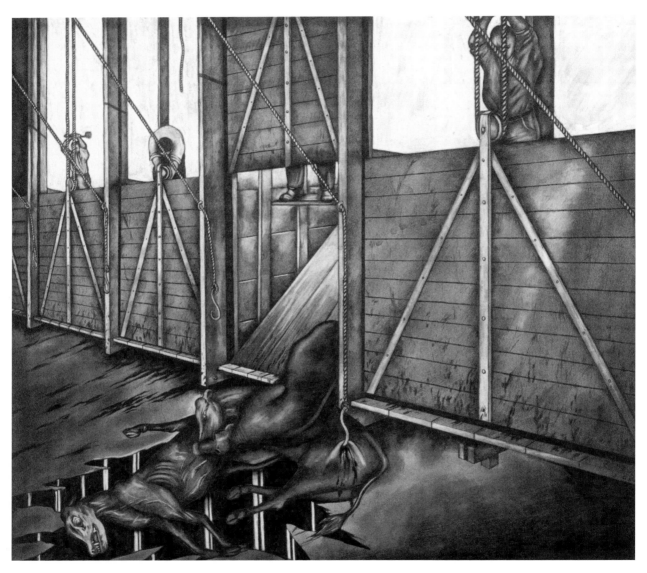

DOG FOOD

E.A. MILLER, BLUE RIBBON BEEF SLAUGHTERHOUSE—UTAH

I gained access to this slaughterhouse by giving a lecture on the meat industry in Utah. A man from the audience said my work was very "easterncentric," meaning from the East Coast, and I responded with a challenge that he should show me around the western meat industry. I went back to New York. To my surprise, he came through, by introducing me to cattle ranchers and arranging for me to go into one of the large slaughterhouses in Utah. John is a rancher himself and the son-in-law of one of the largest ranchers in the state. We've since become friends. Neither he nor I have changed our opinions about the meat industry, but we have a greater knowledge of our differing cultures and viewpoints.

John made the appointment for us to tour the Millers plant. He has been there many times, as his cattle are slaughtered there, and his father-in-law is a buyer for the company. It is a very hot day. Utah has had drought conditions for seven years. We drive to the slaughterhouse, which has the appearance of a missile base, with armed guards in security uniforms at many outposts. Trucks are unloading cattle, and the drivers are waiting around. I pull my camera out and take some photos. A security guard comes and grabs my camera. John argues with them, stating that Millers had okayed my bringing a camera. I argue with them about the legality of them taking my property—to no avail. They say they will keep my camera until I come back outside. I have my sketchbook though, so not all is lost. We go inside and a supervisor called Debbie, who will be our guide, asks us to change our clothing. We go to a large changing room, where there are rows of helmets, boots, and white coats. I put on a knee-length white coat, rubber boots, a safety helmet, goggles, earplugs, and hair net. Everyone is similarly clothed, so there is an alarming conformity, making each of us indistinguishable from the other. We start to shout, the noise is softened by the earplugs. The goggles create an eerie, unearthly view of things. Our clothing is an armor, which has already separated us (humans) from the animals, whose terrible vulnerability is no second skin and no skin at all.

The company slaughters 200 head an hour and 1,600 a day. They have 11,000 workers with 800 on the packing floor. They refer to this as a "small plant," but it is the largest I have seen. Three hundred fifty workers are on the kill floor itself. Sixty percent of the workers are Spanish-speaking, and 30 percent are women. The cattle travel an average of 400 miles to the slaughterhouse. Forty thousand pounds of meat are exported a week, mostly to Korea, Taiwan, and Japan. Millers is owned by ConAgra, the second biggest packing company in the United States.

I ask Debbie why there are not more women on the kill floor. (I see two.) She says that women are welcome to work the floor, as it's not a question of strength since it is fully automated, but most women choose not to. The majority of workers have white helmets, but there are a significant number with red helmets. I ask why and am told that the average meatpacker has a work-life expectancy of one and a half years. The red helmets are trainees and can be easily watched by supervisors.

We go on to the kill floor, but not the actual killing area. The bosses have forbidden it, using the excuse of safety. But I glimpse it, nonetheless. They are using the captive bolt pistol within a steel box, and the back gate falls on the back of the animal, forcing it inside. It's a .22 calibre cartridge. The animal is thus stunned, then hoisted. The throat is cut, the knife is twisted up (the animal is upside down), and the heart is punctured. The blood goes into a tanker and then into the water supply. Debbie, who does quality control, is at pains to point out that it's not the drinking water. I worry that I wouldn't even know the difference.

The conveyor belt goes very fast. The workers are on elevated platforms and each has a specific task. There is the sound of a siren, and the line stops, the knives are put down. This means that one of the government inspectors has stopped the line. It could be that a fluke worm has been found, a round parasite that lives in the liver. This animal will be consigned to pet food. The siren sounds again and the line starts up. The jobs are boring, repetitive, and dangerous. I duck in and out of swinging carcasses. This becomes an odd, gymnastic ballet to avoid the knives, the blood and guts on the floor, and to find an opening between the carcasses, which are huge and very heavy. They keep on coming at you whether or not you are stuck between them. I get used to pushing these giants away and hope they don't fall on me. There are certain points along the conveyor belt where the carcasses twist, and at these points you go behind a very thick, transparent, green plastic curtain. As the animal twists on the hook, the curtain protects the workers from getting caught, and, I suppose, crushed by the broken-off front legs. If a carcass falls to the floor, it is railed off, inspected, and washed. In a room the size of an airport hanger, I see a conveyer with hundreds of skinned heads, and another line of hundreds of hearts moving along at the same speed. Hearts that were beating only moments before.

This cavernous plant has conveyor belts as far as the eye can see. In one room, the workers are working with inhuman speed on the front and hind quarters, manipulating the carcass, boring around the neck and vertebrae with a knife. The workers bob and weave around the swinging carcasses. They have black back harnesses to keep their arms from coming out of the sockets and have become as machine-like as it is possible to imagine. Each carcass weighs between 600 and 700 pounds (Holsteins are thinner). There are workers on the WIZ table (a table devoted to power tools) attached to an electric knife with a flexible cord.

This is Dante's inferno: steam, noise, blood, smell, and speed. Sprinklers wash off meat, giant vacuum-packing machines use heat to seal twenty-two pieces of flesh a minute. Ground beef is packed into glycol and water, long sausage shapes trundle around to be laser scanned and packaged—retail ready. A computer scans each package to record its destination. Thirty-five thousand boxes a day. I can't imagine a human body doing this much labor, day after day. There are posters all around the walls with encouraging slogans, and I wonder how the workforce feels about them. The message is time is money, and workers should avoid injury as it causes the boss to lose money. Signs: THIS DEPARTMENT HAS WORKED ___ DAYS WITHOUT LOST TIME. AVOID ACCIDENTS ON THE JOB. SAFETY BEGINS HERE. PELIGRO ALTO VOLAJE.

In the packing room, the boxes of meat parts are graded 1-5. The gourmet range is 1. Stuck on the ribs of carcasses is a ticket with the lot number, name of supplier, and weight. USDA CHOICE is printed in blue along the fat. I see a tiny, wizened old man in a large cowboy hat among the boxes. It is the owner himself. The workers refer to him sarcastically as God. When I leave the plant, Debbie tells me that I could earn a living making quick sketches. (I have drawn and sketched through the journey.) She thinks I should get a job as a courtroom artist.

I spent some time drawing a tail cutter, as she sliced the tails off and threw them into a bin. She knew I was drawing her, and she slowed down enough so I could get her movements. Verbal communication was impossible because of the noise and earplugs, but she gave me a wonderful smile of knowing.

As we leave the plant, I see a cow with her back broken, nearly concealed. She was still alive and waiting in the hot sun. I try to go up to her, but the security guards escort me off the premises.

SAUSAGE COUNTER

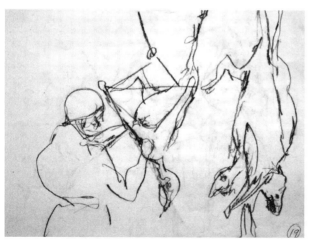

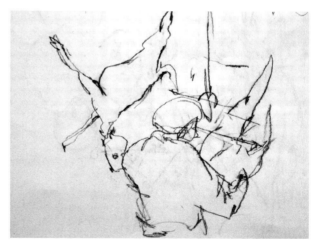

lifting goat

dragging
goat
from
herd to
be killed

JUN 18 1991

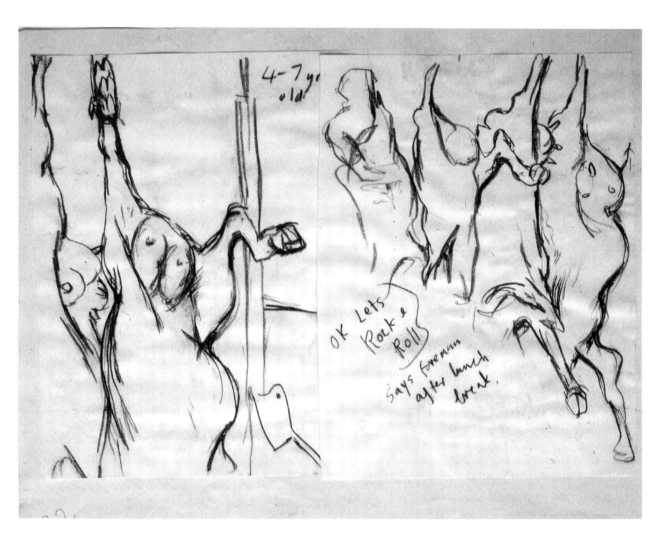

GOATS WAITING
TO BE SLAUGHTERED
TRENTON NJ
JULY 91

BLOOD

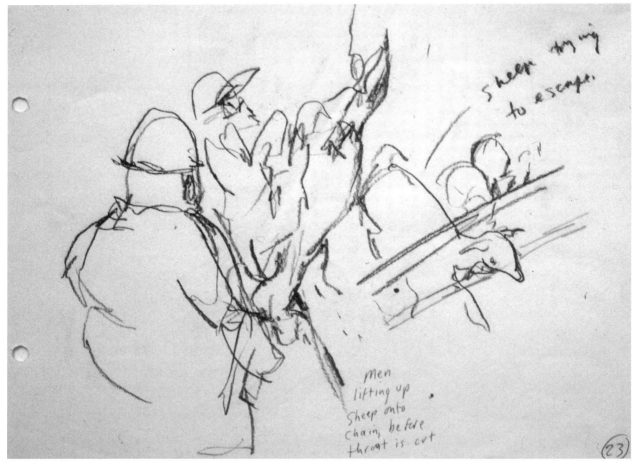

Sheep trying
to escape

Men
lifting up
sheep onto
chains before
throat is cut

I ask Jimmy about politics.
He says he doesnt ever think about
it. He says that he gets
unemployment - and works off
the books - a cash job.
Jimmy works as a DJ on
weekends, his favorite bands
are Led Zep & Public Enemy.
He wants a car, and tells
me he had a cellular phone
like all his friends - but the first
bill was $350, so he got rid of it.
His brother is getting married
at age 28 - the whole
family will go to Greece for the wedding.
Jimmy wonders when he
will get a girlfriend, if he
says he doesnt care. He's 21 years old,
never gets one.
Jimmy shares his ciggr
with me, and soda. He wants....
he doesnt want to do this
job - its heavy lifting and
doesnt pay enough. When we
go to look at the killing floor
he jokes about it, but then gets
upset - "Its wrong". I am amazed
as he handles the dead corpses
all day, that he hasnt seen the
killing.

They work, its
repetitive motion,
a hundred veals, hung
and skinned.

I look at
the skinners hand
there is something
wrong, I look more
closely and each
finger has been
severed at the
joint, stumps
only. He has
and thumb.

Jimmy
unloading
veals.

MONTREAL MAY 91

Montreal May 91

15

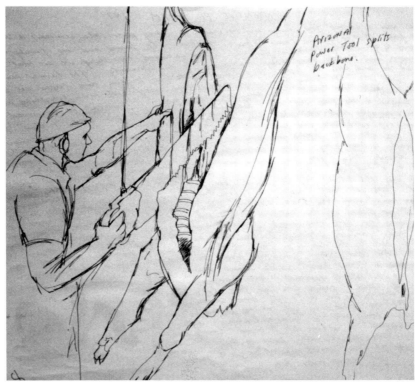

Arizona!
Power Tool splits
backbone.

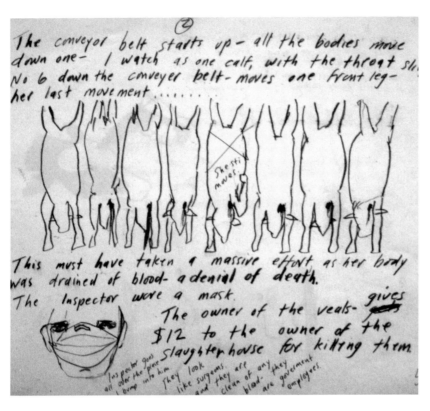

The conveyor belt starts up — all the bodies move down one — I watch as one calf, with the throat sl... No 6 down the conveyer belt — moves one front leg — her last movement ....

She sti... moves

This must have taken a massive effort, as her body was drained of blood — a denial of death.

The Inspector wore a mask.

The owner of the veals — gives $12 to the owner of the slaughterhouse for killing them.

Inspector goes all over the place. I bump into him. They look like surgeons and they are clean of any blood. They are government employees.

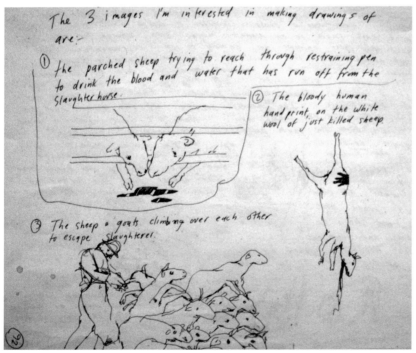

The 3 images I'm interested in making drawings of are:

① the parched sheep trying to reach through restraining pen to drink the blood and water that has run off from the slaughterhouse.

② The bloody human hand print on the white wool of just killed sheep.

③ The sheep & goats climbing over each other to escape slaughterer.

veal calves about to be slaughtered

back steel plate of holding pen, repeatedly
dropped down on backs of calves — to
'pursuade' them to move forward —
heard the crashing on their bones.
A few feet away is the throat cutting
this looks more like a hole in
the throat — the blood comes
out like solid black/red glass.
steam comes out of the slit
bodied — I see bits of flesh where
I'm standing.

Montreal
April '91

①

Veal calf is
3-4 months old
at slaughter —
weighs 230-300

(The bosses wont let me draw/photo in
slaughter house — so wrote this day later)

5.

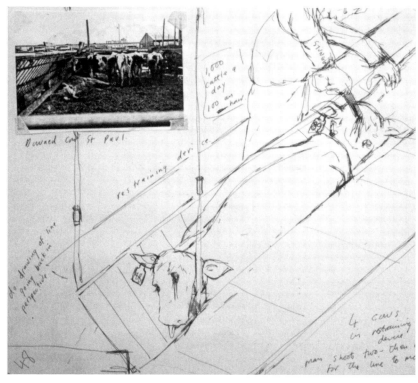

Downed Cow St Paul.

restraining device

1,600
cattle a
day
180 an
hour

do drawing of line
going back in
perspective

4 cows
in restraining
device
man shoots two — then
for the line to run

3.

We watch a worker scoop the brains out of a skull—thats his only job. We look into a giant vat its full of brains. Maybe 300 brains—they look larger than human brains. They are white with blood clots. We look into another vat and The Jobber tells me—thats all livers.

They are v. large yellow he says, yellow liquid comes out of them, which means they have been pumped up (Hormones).

40 full time (Workers (Union) get $15 an hour (Canadian) kill 1000 head a week - to 3000

(WORKERS MAKE 1,500 cuts an hour)

There is a long line of workers as far as the eye can see they cut meat off bones, ribs etc. They work so FAST I cant see their hands moving.

Jobber get 10cents on the lb. HoT Meat— is meat which hasnt hung for 72 hours

55

stockyard worker kicking and whipping a downed cult

Including cows with cancer, this cow— half her face had been eaten away. It's not in the farmers finan... interest to euthanize an animal that can still gain weight— or produce...

She is frothing at the mouth— and is thin, with her one eye, she looks at m... what seems like sadness. She just w... Cancer had eaten away— her eye, and p... her skull and brain. The white fr... her mouth turns into icicles.

I pick up different types of teeth, j... dust, cow teeth, and hogs teeth. that had been beaten out, a or ... out. This place, which must ... hundred years old— seems ful... millions of ghosts of animals— wh... passed through here— now forgo... Steam from hot bodies rises into ... along with breath. A truck ba... and hogs are being unloaded, the... whipping and beating them, to get... to move faster. All the animals f... and start to move back in their...

Cow with cancer of the eye

LIVERPOOL SLAUGHTERHOUSE

Ecolait Montreal

lived their short lives in a crate, and only given milk to drink – no roughage to build bones. So their bones can't hold them. Veals are usually caked with diarrhea on their fur. The person on the other side of the steal retraining crate, is getting frustrated because the veals wont move inside. They are ⅔ of the way in. The door keeps dropping down on them from above. It's a steel door. It keeps rising up and dropping down. It winches up, and then falls down on their backs, hitting them again & again. So the veals are getting electrocuted from behind, and smashed from above – they move into the crate. This crate and them being squished together prevents any movement. I can see in their ears are stapled their lot numbers. They look around wildly, making no sound, their heads are trembling like with palsy. White foam is dripping out of their mouths. One calf looks at me with what appears to be trust in humans. They wait. The worker with the either the bolt pistol or the electro lethalizer (I am not sure which, as I was watching the calves) runs one hand from the head of the calf, right down to the flank. I am mesmerized by this action, so much so, that I didn't see him shoot the calves. We are standing in the 2nd stage of the killing – the "STICKING." I look down, and I am standing 63

132   SUE COE

The Downer is too heavy to get up. She cries as her chain is attached to her leg - and a winch drags her along the ground to a truck. I can see the skin wear off, and the bones grind into the pavement. She cant lift her head up - the stone. and eye, start to tear on the head, ear look at the man. he looks impatient. As her bones become the ground, I see point on the bone, with the white blood. I start to think of school songs - see my eyes still brain but my is occupied -

all we sang at school grinding religeous ditties - There is a green hill far away

Fucking biblical garbage

As she reaches the truck -

She semi rolls over exposing her uddess: which are full of milk - this is the total degredation of a life.

being dragged to slaughter stockyard

She cries as she is dragged along.

PENN

144

Tiny calf, left without food and water at stockyard in St Paul - its Sunday - 95°. She struggles to get up (I think her back might be broken) white froth is coming out of her mouth. She makes one last attempt, but the movement throws her head back, which now seems too heavy for her neck, and then she is still.

dying calf at stockyard

April 91

pit- like a sand pit, with no sand. The neck goes into the pit gushing blood.
The animal goes thin like a pencil- just fur and ~~fur~~ a skeleton. His legs still are
running. And continue to do so for some time. The 2nd goat is grabbed and the
proceedure is repeated. The floor is covered
with blood, I can see my reflection in it.
On the walls are saws, and knives, and
different pullies.

blood drains into pit.

One sheep is let in. She is white- with
a blue brand on her side, and black feet.
The door closes. She runs around the kill floor-
the workers seem to forget her, they are not ~~know~~ in the killing pen
but over by the skinning table having a conversation in whispers. The foreman
comes over and says, not to put any of their faces in my pictures. The
sheep waits, her hooves and legs are covered with blood. The door
opens again, and 2 sheep are pushed
in- the outside worker doesn't know
the killing has stopped. The sheep
start to bleat. (bleet?) terrible
soft sounds.

~~Pit~~ Piteous
cries. The sound
falls out of the
thick air, as though
it never was.

Steaming water from ~~her~~ hoses, runs the old blood away down
the drain. And the killing starts again. I'm glad
Santiago is there, although I barely know him. I feel responsible
for putting him in this situation. I see, what is going on

Sticking

Skinning

He says to me "I don't
think of these animals
as living beings, I think
of them, as a librarian
thinks of books,
as an auto worker
thinks of
car parts,
this is, a
factory"

136

② Farmer Johns L.A.

On our second visit, we gain entrance - unnoticed. Inside the walls are large buildings doing processing, and many trucks unloading into outside pens. Then the hogs are electric prodded into the slaughter house. There are many CRIPS and dying and dead hogs. That have been seperated and are just waiting in the yard, some sitting in their own blood. They are different hogs from the ones I usually see on the East Coast. They are beautiful, with huge heads and snouts, and quite small bodies - can see the ribs. The hogs are driven through - a stampede - leaving behind the ones that cant walk, or are dead.
Sitting in blood & urine.

The suffering of these animals cannot be described - they are bleeding from the mouth and nose - could have broken backs - and can be left in the heat for days - without water, until they die - or are dragged into the slaughter house. They are called DOWNERS by the industry.

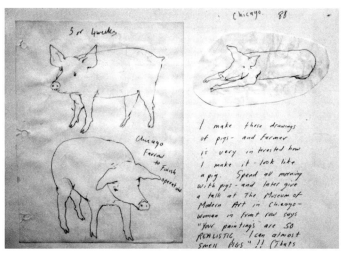

Chicago 88

3 or 4 weeks

Chicago Farms to finish operation

I make these drawings of pigs - and farmer is very interested how I make it look like a pig. Spend all morning with pigs - and later give a talk at the Museum of Modern Art in Chicago - woman in front row says "Your paintings are so REALISTIC, I can almost smell pigs" !! (Thats

I forgot, after the throat has been cut the man goes over to the hose, and rinses off his hands and arms— so the knife won't slip.